SpringerBriefs in Electrical and Computer Engineering

Series Editors

Stan Zdonik
Peng Ning
Shashi Shekhar
Jonathan Katz
Xindong Wu
Lakhmi C. Jain
David Padua
Xuemin Shen
Borko Furht
V. S. Subrahmanian
Martial Hebert
Katsushi Ikeuchi
Bruno Siciliano

T0205964

For further volumes:
http://www.springer.com/series/10059

Nikos Manouselis · Hendrik Drachsler
Katrien Verbert · Erik Duval

Recommender Systems
for Learning

Nikos Manouselis
Agro-Know Technologies
Athens
Greece

Hendrik Drachsler
Open University of the Netherlands
Heerlen
The Netherlands

Katrien Verbert
KU Leuven
Leuven
Belgium

Erik Duval
KU Leuven
Leuven
Belgium

ISSN 2191-8112   ISSN 2191-8120   (electronic)
ISBN 978-1-4614-4360-5   ISBN 978-1-4614-4361-2   (eBook)
DOI 10.1007/978-1-4614-4361-2
Springer New York Heidelberg Dordrecht London

Library of Congress Control Number: 2012940235

© The Authors 2013
This work is subject to copyright. All rights are reserved by the Publisher, whether the whole or part of the material is concerned, specifically the rights of translation, reprinting, reuse of illustrations, recitation, broadcasting, reproduction on microfilms or in any other physical way, and transmission or information storage and retrieval, electronic adaptation, computer software, or by similar or dissimilar methodology now known or hereafter developed. Exempted from this legal reservation are brief excerpts in connection with reviews or scholarly analysis or material supplied specifically for the purpose of being entered and executed on a computer system, for exclusive use by the purchaser of the work. Duplication of this publication or parts thereof is permitted only under the provisions of the Copyright Law of the Publisher's location, in its current version, and permission for use must always be obtained from Springer. Permissions for use may be obtained through RightsLink at the Copyright Clearance Center. Violations are liable to prosecution under the respective Copyright Law.
The use of general descriptive names, registered names, trademarks, service marks, etc. in this publication does not imply, even in the absence of a specific statement, that such names are exempt from the relevant protective laws and regulations and therefore free for general use.
While the advice and information in this book are believed to be true and accurate at the date of publication, neither the authors nor the editors nor the publisher can accept any legal responsibility for any errors or omissions that may be made. The publisher makes no warranty, express or implied, with respect to the material contained herein.

Printed on acid-free paper

Springer is part of Springer Science+Business Media (www.springer.com)

Preface

Recommender systems are extremely popular as a research and application area, with various interesting application domains such as e-commerce, entertainment, and others. Nevertheless, it was only around early 2000 when the first notable applications appeared in the domain of education, since relevant work was generally considered to be connected to the area of adaptive educational systems.

Today, research around recommender systems in an educational context has significantly increased. Responding to a growing interest, this book expands the relevant chapter on Recommender Systems in Technology Enhanced Learning (by Manouselis, Drachsler, Vuorikari, Hummel and Koper) that was published in the Springer Recommender Systems Handbook (2011) to provide an extensive and in-depth analysis of the recommender systems currently found in the relevant literature. The book briefly introduces recommender systems for learning and discusses a wide and representative sample of issues that people working on systems should be expecting to face. It serves as an overview of work in this domain and therefore especially addresses people who are studying or researching relevant topics and want to position their work in the overall landscape.

The bibliography covered by this book is available in an open group created at the Mendeley research platform[1] and will continue to be enriched with additional references. We would like to encourage the reader to sign up for this group and to connect to the community of people working on these topics, gaining access to the

---

[1] http://www.mendeley.com/groups/1969281/recommender-systems-for-learning/

collected blibliography but also contributing pointers to new relevant publications within this very fast emerging domain.

We hope that you will enjoy reading this book as much as we enjoyed working on it.

Nikos Manouselis
Hendrik Drachsler
Katrien Verbert
Erik Duval

Acknowledgments

We would like to thank all the people who have inspired this work and contributed to the discussion around these topics in various fora and opportunities. Particular appreciation is reserved for our co-authors of the chapter upon which this work has developed and expanded: Riina Vuorikari, Hans Hummel, and Rob Koper. We also thank Laura Gavrilut for her support in proof-reading the final version of the book.

The work presented in this book has been carried out with European Commission funding support. More specifically, the work of Nikos Manouselis has been supported by the EU projects CIP PSP VOA3R (http://www.voa3r.eu) and FP7 agINFRA (http://www.aginfra.eu). The work of Hendrik Drachsler was funded by the NeLLL funding body in the context of the AlterEgo project. Katrien Verbert is a Postdoctoral Fellow of the Research Foundation Flanders (FWO). Part of this work was also supported by the SIG dataTEL of the European Association of Technology Enhanced Learning and the former dataTEL Theme Team of the STELLAR Network of Excellence (grant agreement no. 231913). This publication reflects the views only of the authors, and the funding bodies and agencies cannot be held responsible for any use that may be made of the information contained therein.

Contents

Acronyms

AEH	Adaptive Educational Hypermedia
CAM	Contextualised Attention Metadata
CSCL	Computer Supported Collaborative Learning
EDM	Educational Data Mining
IR	Information Retrieval
ITS	Intelligent Tutoring System
KSA	Knowledge, Skills, Abilities
LAK	Learning and Knowledge Analytics
LMS	Learning Management System
LOM	Learning Object Metadata
MCDM	Multi-Criteria Decision Making
MUPPLE	Mash-Up Personal Learning Environment
OAI	Open Archives Initiative
PSLC	Pittsburgh Science of Learning Center
TEL	Technology Enhanced Learning
VLE	Virtual Learning Environments

Chapter 1
Introduction and Background

Abstract In this chapter, we start with a short introduction to the increase that has been witnessed in the past few years in applications of recommender systems at the TEL domain. Then we provide some background on the area of recommender systems, by defining recommender systems and outlining their basic types. A comparison with relevant work in TEL is tried, particularly focusing on adaptive educational hypermedia, learning networks, educational data mining, and learning analytics. A discussion on their similarities and differences is also made, so that relevant work can be better positioned in the TEL research landscape.

1.1 Introduction

Technology enhanced learning (TEL) aims to design, develop and test sociotechnical innovations that will support and enhance learning practices of both individuals and organisations. It is therefore an application domain that generally covers technologies that support all forms of teaching and learning activities. Since information retrieval (in terms of searching for relevant learning resources to support teachers or learners) is a pivotal activity in TEL, the deployment of recommender systems has attracted increased interest.

This should be more or less expected since a traditional problem in TEL has been the better findability of (mainly) digital learning resources. For instance, digital learning content is being regularly produced, organised and published in different types of TEL environments such as (Ochoa 2011):

1. *Learning Object Repositories* like Learning Resource Exchange,[1] Connexions[2] or Maricopa Exchange[3];

---

[1] http://lreforschools.eun.org

[2] http://cnx.org

[3] http://www.mcli.dist.maricopa.edu/mlx/

N. Manouselis et al., *Recommender Systems for Learning*,
SpringerBriefs in Electrical and Computer Engineering,
DOI: 10.1007/978-1-4614-4361-2_1, © The Authors 2013

2. *Learning Object Referratories* like MERLOT,[4] OER Commons[5] or GLOBE[6];
3. *Open Courseware* sites like MIT OCW[7] or OpenLearn[8];
4. *Learning Management Systems* and Course Management Systems like Blackboard[9] and Moodle[10].

Various opportunities emerge for users to be exposed to this plethora of digital learning resources, in closed communities or in public, and in both formal and non-formal settings. Potentially all user groups of TEL systems would find attractive services that help them identify suitable learning resources from this overwhelming variety of choices. As a consequence, the concept of recommender systems became extremely appealing for TEL research. This is also reflected in the increasing networking and publication activities of researchers working on such applications. Recent examples include the Workshop series of Social Information Retrieval for Technology Enhanced Learning (SIRTEL2007–2009), the RecSysTEL Workshop on Recommender Systems for Technology Enhanced Learning (Manouselis et al. 2010), the 1st dataTEL workshop on data sets for Technology Enhanced Learning (Drachsler et al. 2010b, to appear), and several relevant special volumes of journals and books (Vuorikari et al. 2009; Verbert et al. 2010; Santos and Boticario 2012, in press; Tang et al. to appear). These efforts resulted in a number of interesting observations, the main ones being that:

a) There is a large number of recommender systems that have been deployed (or that are currently under deployment) in TEL settings;
b) The information retrieval goals that TEL recommenders try to achieve are often different to the ones identified in other systems (e.g. product recommenders);
c) There is a need to identify the particularities of TEL recommender systems, in order to elaborate on methods for their systematic design, development and evaluation.

Attempting to explore such particularities of this application domain, our book extends the analysis of Manouselis et al. (2011) in order to make a somewhat comprehensive introduction of how recommender systems are deployed in TEL settings. Its main contribution is that it discusses a wide and representative set of issues that people working on recommender systems for learning should be expecting to face. It does not serve as an exhaustive review and analysis of available approaches and systems, but gives a rather fair overview of work in this domain.

The remainder of this book is structured as follows. This chapter introduces recommender systems and discusses their relevance to similar areas in TEL. Chapter 2

---

[4] http://www.merlot.org

[5] http://www.oercommons.org

[6] http://globe-info.org

[7] http://ocw.mit.edu

[8] http://openlearn.open.ac.uk

[9] http://www.blackboard.com

[10] http://moodle.org

focuses more on describing TEL as a recommendation context, defining the TEL recommendation problem and identifying relevant goals, supported user tasks, and variables of the TEL context that can be considered when making a recommendation. It also reviews data sets that are currently available from TEL applications and discusses how they could be useful for research on TEL recommender systems. Chapter 3 offers a comprehensive analysis of 42 recommender systems that have been found in relevant literature. Chapter 4 describes current challenges in the field and gives an outlook of future research trends in TEL recommender systems.

1.2 Recommender Systems

1.2.1 Definitions

Malone et al. (1987) provided an overview of intelligent information sharing systems, referring to a fundamental categorisation of systems that generally support access to highly dynamic information resources (Belkin and Croft 1992; Baudisch 2001; Hanani et al. 2001). More specifically, they distinguished cognitive filtering systems as the ones that characterise the contents of an information resource (shortly referred to as an item) and the information needs of potential item users, and then use these representations to intelligently match items to users; and sociological filtering systems as the ones that are working based on the personal and organisational interrelationships of individuals in a community. Early information sharing systems belonged to the first category and were based on text-based filtering, which works by selecting relevant items according to a set of textual keywords (Konstan 2004). Collaborative filtering systems were first introduced as representatives of the second category. They addressed two problems of text-based systems:

- The problem of overwhelming numbers of on-topic items (ones which would be all selected by a keyword filter), which has been addressed by the introduction of further evaluating the items based on human judgment about their quality.
- The problem of filtering non-text items, which has been addressed by judging them solely upon human taste.

Therefore, early recommender systems were based on the notion of collaborative filtering, and have been defined as systems that ". . .help people make choices based on the opinions of other people." (Goldberg et al. 1992). As years came by, the term "recommender systems" has prevailed over the term "collaborative filtering systems". It first described systems in which ". . .people provide recommendations as inputs, which the system then aggregates and directs to appropriate recipients." (Resnick and Varian 1997). Finally, it evolved to a meaning that is more or less valid today, covering ". . .any system that produces individualised recommendations as output or has the effect of guiding the user in a personalised way to interesting or useful objects in a large space of possible options."

Table 1.1 Overview of definitions related to recommender systems

Goldberg et al. (1992)	"Collaborative filtering simply means that people collaborate to help one anotherperform filtering by recording their reactions to documents they read."
Resnick et al. (1994)	"Collaborative filters help people make choices based on the opinions of other people."
Shardanand and Maes (1995)	"Social information filtering essentially automates the process of 'word-of-mouth' recommendations: items are recommended to a user based upon values assigned by other people with similar taste."
Resnick and Varian (1997)	"In a typical recommender system people provide recommendations as inputs, which the system then aggregates and directs to appropriate recipients."
Pennock and Horvitz (1999); Goldberg et al. (2001)	"The term 'collaborative filtering' describes techniques that use the known preferences of a group of users to predict the unknown preferences of a new user; recommendations for the new users are based on these predictions. Other terms that have been proposed are 'social information filtering' and 'recommender system'."
Schafer et al. (2001)	"Recommender systems use product knowledge -either hand-coded knowledge provided by experts or 'mined' knowledge learned from the behavior of consumers- to guide consumers through the often-overwhelming task of locating products they will like."
Burke (2002); Lops et al. (2011)	"...any system that produces individualised recommendations as output or has the effect of guiding the user in a personalized way to interesting or useful objects in a large space of possible options."
Konstan (2004)	"Recommender systems use the opinions of members of a community to help individuals in that community identify the information or products most likely to be interesting to them or relevant to their needs."
Herlocker et al. (2004)	"Recommender systems use the opinions of a community of users to help individuals in that community more effectively identify content of interest from a potentially overwhelmingset of choices."
Deshpande and Karypis (2004)	"Recommender systems—a personalized information filtering technology used to either predict whether a particular user will like a particular item (prediction problem) or to identify aset of N items that will be of interest to a certain user (top-N recommendation problem)."
Hung (2005)	"A personalized recommendation system can provide one-to-one service to customers based on customers' past behavior and through inference from other users with similar preferences. The aim of personalization is to offer customers what they want without asking explicitly and to capture the social component of inter-personal interaction."
Schein et al. (2005)	"Recommender systems suggest items of interest to users based on their explicit and implicit preferences, the preferences of other users, and user and item attributes."
Smyth (2007)	"Recommender systems try to help users access complex information spaces."

(continued)

Table 1.1 (continued)

Burke (2007)	"Recommender systems are personalized information agents that provide recommendations: suggestions for items likely to be of use to a user... A recommender can be distinguished from an information retrieval system by the semantics of its user interaction."
Ekstrand et al. (2010)	"...other users' opinions can be selected and aggregated in such a way as to provide a reasonable prediction of the active user's preference."

(Burke 2002; Burke and Ramezani 2011). Even though this definition covers also the classic text-based filtering systems, Burke (2002) states that two criteria distinguish recommender systems from text-based ones: the criterion of 'individualised' and the criterion of 'interesting and useful' content. Table 1.1 provides an overview of relevant definitions that we have identified in the literature, extending the initial collection reported in Manouselis and Costopoulou (2007).

1.2.2 Types

In the literature, recommender systems have been usually classified into two basic types, according to the way recommendations are made (Adomavicius and Tuzhilin 2005):

- *Content-based recommendation*, in which the user is recommended items similar to the ones he has preferred in the past. Content-based recommendation systems analyse a set of items and/or descriptions previously preferred by a user, and build a model or profile of user interests based on the features of these items (Lops et al. 2011; Pazzani and Billsus 1997).
- *Collaborative recommendation*, in which the user is recommended items that people with similar tastes and preferences liked in the past. Collaborative recommendation (or collaborative filtering) systems predict a user's interest in new items based on the recommendations of other people with similar interests (Schafer et al. 2007; Ekstrand et al. 2010).

Moreover, other types of recommender systems have been also proposed in the literature. For instance, Burke (2002, 2007) distinguishes the following ones (in addition to the two described above):

- *Demographic recommendation*, which classifies the users according to the attributes of their personal profile, and makes recommendations based on demographic classes.
- *Utility-based recommendation*, which makes suggestions based on a computation of the utility of each item for a user, for whom a utility function has to be stored.

- *Knowledge-based recommendation*, which suggests items based on logical inferences about user preferences. A knowledge representation (e.g. rules) about how
  an item meets a particular user need is necessary.

Furthermore, Adomavicius and Tuzhilin (2005) also distinguish recommenders in
those that aim to predict absolute values of ratings users would give to yet unseen
items, from preference-based filtering, i.e. predicting the relative preferences of users.
Finally, hybrid recommendation has also been identified. Recommender systems of
this type combine two or more of the aforementioned types in order to gain better
performance and address the shortcomings of each type (Burke 2002; 2007).

1.3 Relevant Systems in Educational Applications

1.3.1 Adaptive Educational Hypermedia

Web systems generally suffer from the inability to satisfy the heterogeneous needs
of many users. To address this challenge, a particular strand of research that has
been called adaptive web systems (or adaptive hypermedia) tried to overcome the
shortcomings of traditional 'one-size-fits-all' approaches by exploring ways in which
Web-based systems could adapt their behaviour to the goals, tasks, interests, and
other characteristics of interested users (Brusilovsky and Nejdl 2004). A particular
category of adaptive systems has been the one dealing with educational applications,
called adaptive educational hypermedia (AEH) systems.

Adaptive web systems belong to the class of user-adaptive software systems
(Schneider-Hufschmidt et al. 1993). According to Oppermann (1994) a system is
called adaptive "if it is able to change its own characteristics automatically according to the user's needs". Adaptive systems consider the way the user interacts with the
system and modify the interface presentation or the system behaviour accordingly
(Weibelzahl 2003). Jameson (2001) adds an important characteristic: a user-adaptive
system is an interactive system which adapts its behaviour to each individual user on
the basis of nontrivial inferences from information about that user.

Adaptive systems help users find relevant items in a usually large information
space, by essentially engaging three main adaptation technologies (Brusilovsky and
Nejdl 2004): adaptive content selection, adaptive navigation support, and adaptive
presentation. The first of these three technologies comes from the field of adaptive
information retrieval (IR) (Baudisch 2001) and is associated with a search-based
access to information. When the user searches for relevant information, the system
can adaptively select and prioritise the most relevant items. The second technology
was introduced by adaptive hypermedia systems (Brusilovsky 1996) and is associated
with a browsing-based access to information. When the user navigates from one item
to another, the system can manipulate the links (e.g. hide, sort, annotate) to guide
the user adaptively to most relevant information items. The third technology has its
roots in the research on adaptive explanation and adaptive presentation in intelligent

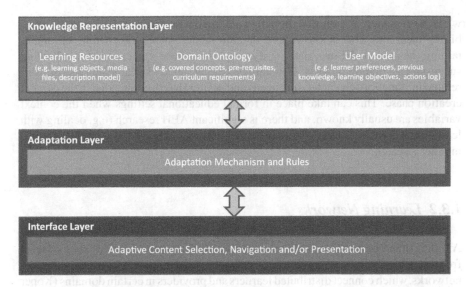

Fig. 1.1 Generic layers within a simplified example architecture of an educational AEH (adapted from: Karampiperis and Sampson 2005; Manouselis et al. 2011)

systems (Moore and Swartout 1990; Paris 1988). It deals with presentation, not access to information. When the user gets to a particular page, the system can present its content adaptively.

As Brusilovsky (2001) describes, educational hypermedia was one of the first application areas of adaptive systems. A simplified architecture of the layers within an educational AEH system that has been developed simplifying the elaborate one found in Karampiperis and Sampson (2005) is presented in Fig. 1.1. This architecture includes: a layer including the representation and organisation of knowledge about educational content (learning resources), the domain (domain ontology), and the user (user model); a layer that includes the adaptation mechanisms and rules; and a layer that provides the run-time adaptation results to the user. A number of pioneer adaptive educational hypermedia systems were developed between 1990 and 1996, which Brusilovksy roughly divided into two research streams. The first stream includes systems created by researchers in the area of intelligent tutoring systems (ITS) who were trying to extend traditional student modelling and adaptation approaches developed in this field to ITS with hypermedia components (Brusilovsky et al. 1993; Gonschorek and Herzog 1995; Prez et al. 1995). The systems of the second stream were developed by researchers working on educational hypermedia in an attempt to make their systems adapt to individual students (De Bra 1996; De La Passardiere and Dufresne 1992; Hohl, Böcker and Gunzenhäuser 1996; Kay and Kummerfeld 1994).

AEH research has often followed a top-down approach, greatly depending on expert knowledge and involvement in order to identify and model TEL context variables. For example, Cristea (2005) describes a number of expertise-demanding tasks when AEH content is authored: initially creating the resources, labeling them, combining them into what is known as a domain model; then, constructing and maintaining the user model in a static or dynamic way, since it is crucial for achieving successful adaptation in AEH. Generally speaking, in AEH a large amount of user-related information (characterising needs and desires) has to be encoded in the content creation phase. This can take place in formal educational settings when the context variables are usually known, and there is significant AEH research (e.g. dealing with learner and domain models) that can be considered and reused within TEL recommender research.

1.3.2 Learning Networks

Another strand of work includes research where the context variables are extracted from the contributions of the users. A category of such systems includes learning networks, which connect distributed learners and providers in certain domains (Koper and Tattersall 2004; Koper et al. 2005). The design and development of learning networks is highly flexible, learner-centric and evolving from the bottom upwards, going beyond formal course and programme-centric models that are imposed from the top downwards. A learning network is populated with many learners and learning activities provided by different stakeholders. Each user is allowed to add, edit, delete or evaluate learning resources at any time.

The concept of learning networks (Koper et al. 2005) provides methods and technical infrastructures for distributed lifelong learners to support their personal competence development. It takes advantages of the possibilities of the Web 2.0 developments and describes the new dynamics of learning in the networked knowledge society. A learning network is learner-centered and its development emerges from the bottom-up through the participation of the learners. Emergence is the central idea of the learning network concept. Emergence appears when an interacting system of individual actors and resources self-organises to shape higher-level patterns of behaviour (Gordon 1999; Johnson 2001; Waldrop 1992).

We can imagine users (e.g. learners) interacting with learning activities in a learning network while their progress is being recorded. Indirect measures like time or learning outcomes, and direct measures like ratings and tags given by users allow to identify paths in a learning network which are faster to complete or more attractive than others (e.g. Drachsler 2009a; Vuorikari and Koper 2009). This information can be fed back to other learners in the learning network, providing collective knowledge of the 'swarm of learners' in the learning network. Most learning environments are designed only top-down as often times their structure, learning activities and learning routes are predefined by an educational institution (Fig. 1.2). Learning networks, on the other hand, take advantage of the user-generated content that is created, shared, rated and adjusted by using Web 2.0 technologies. In the field of TEL, several European projects address these bottom-up approaches of creating and sharing

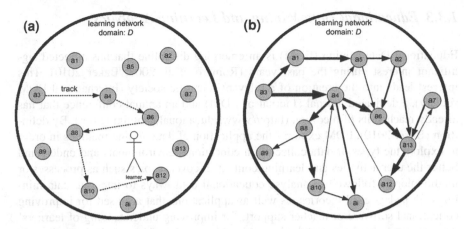

Fig. 1.2 Evolution of a learning network from Drachsler et al. (2009b) (*left* **A** starting phase with a first learner moving through possible learning activities; *right* **B** advanced phase showing emerging learning paths from the collective behavior of all learners)

knowledge, such as the TENcompetence project (Wilson et al. 2008) or the LTfLL project (Drachsler et al. 2010a).

Following a similar approach, in Research Networks researchers are interconnected over Web 2.0 tools and are informed about latest research activities. This combined information of a specific research community easily becomes overwhelming, thus also researchers face an information overflow issue. Customised awareness support tools are needed to visualise and explore the collected data. But also recommender systems are becoming increasingly important to support researchers in the daily work process (Reinhardt et al. 2011a,b).

Another category of systems that formulate and define their context variables following a bottom-up approach, are Mash-Up Personal Learning Environments (MUPPLE) (Wild et al. 2008). First such approaches were created by Liber (2000); Liber and Johnson (2008); Wild et al. (2008). The iCamp EU-initiative explicitly addresses the integration of Web 2.0 sources into MUPPLE, by creating a flexible environment that allows learners to create their own environments for certain learning activities. MUPPLEs are a kind of instance of the learning network concept and therefore share several characteristics with it. They also support informal learning as they require no institutional background and focus on the learner instead of institutional needs like student management or assessments. The learners do not participate in formal courses and neither receive any certification for their competence development. A common problem for MUPPLEs is the amount of data that is gathered already in a short time frame and the unstructured way it is collected. This can make the process of user and domain modelling demanding and unstructured. On the other hand, this is often the case in recommender systems as well, when user and item interactions are explored, e.g. in order to identify user and item similarities.

1.3.3 Educational Data Mining and Learning Analytics

Educational Data Mining (EDM) is an emerging discipline that has attracted significant interest during the past years (Romero et al. 2008; Baker 2010). This interest leads into the creation of a relevant scientific society (International EDM society), a dedicated journal (Journal of EDM) and an annual conference that has already reached its fifth edition (http://www.educationaldatamining.org). By definition (Baker 2010), EDM explores the application of data mining methods in order to explore the types of data collected in educational environments and understand better the user activities and learning context. It covers topics such as processes or methodologies followed to analyse educational data, ways to integrate data mining with pedagogical theories, as well as applications that are used for improving educational software or teacher support, for improving understanding of learners' domain representations, and for improving assessment of learners' engagement in the learning tasks.

Traditional data mining methods are used to support mining educational data sets, but trying to discover and take advantage of the unique features of educational data. Baker and Yacef (2010) classified the EDM areas into: prediction (e.g. classification, regression, density estimation); clustering; relationship mining (e.g. association rule mining, correlation mining, sequential pattern mining, causal data mining); distillation of data for human judgment; and discovery with models. In EDM, whether educational data is taken from students' use of interactive learning environments, computer-supported collaborative learning, or administrative data from schools and universities, it often has multiple levels of meaningful hierarchy, which often need to be determined by properties in the data itself, rather than in advance. Furthermore, issues of time, sequence, and context also play important roles in the study of educational data. The work in this area can be considered to be relevant to the domain of recommender systems for educational applications, since many recommender systems apply data mining techniques in order to cluster users, find correlations and improve their recommendations (Romero and Ventura 2010).

In addition, an emerging strand of research is around the topic of the so-called Learning and Knowledge Analytics (LAK), as reflected by a number of conferences and special issues in recent years (Siemens 2010; Siemens and Gasevic 2011). Among others, the analysis of learner data and identification of patterns within these data are researched to predict learning outcomes, to suggest relevant resources and to detect error patterns or affects of learners. The definition of Learning Analytics by Siemens (2010) describes them as the use of intelligent data, learner-produced data, and analysis models to discover information and social connections, and to predict and advise on learning. This definition reveals that Learning Analytics are very closely related to EDM, with a particular emphasis on knowledge representation and reasoning (Romero and Ventura 2007). This is perfectly justified since, in an increasing number of scientific disciplines, large data collections are emerging as important community resources (Chervenak et al. 2000). These data sets are used as benchmarks to develop new algorithms and compare them to other algorithms in given settings. For instance, when data sets are intended to be used for recommendations algorithms, various data types such as explicit (ratings) or implicit (downloads and tags) can serve as potential relevance indicators.

1.3.4 Similarities and Differences

Many of the AEH systems address formal learning (e.g. Aroyo et al. 2003; De Bra et al. 2002; Kravcik et al. 2004), have equally fine granulated knowledge domains and can therefore offer personalised recommendations to the learners. They take advantage of technologies like metadata and ontologies to define the relationships, conditions, and dependencies of learning resources and learner models. These systems are mainly used in 'closed-corpus' applications (Brusilovsky and Henze 2007) where the learning resources can be described by an educational designer through semantic relationships and is therefore a formal learning offer. As mentioned before, in formal educational settings (such as universities) there are usually well- structured formal relationships like predefined learning plans (curriculum) with locations, student/teacher profiles, and accreditation procedures. All this metadata can be used to recommend courses or personalise learning through the adaptation of the learning resources or the learning environment to the students (Baldoni et al. 2007). One interesting direction in this research is the work on adaptive sequencing which takes into account individual characteristics and preferences for sequencing learning resources (Karampiperis and Sampson 2005). In AEH there are many design activities needed before the runtime and also during the maintenance of the learning environment. In addition, the knowledge domains in the learning environment need to be described in detail. These aspects make adaptive sequencing and other adaptive hypermedia techniques less applicable for TEL recommendation, where informal learning networks emerge without some highly structured domain model representation.

In informal learning networks, mining techniques need to be used in order to create some representation of the user or domain model. For instance, prior knowledge in informal learning is a rather diffuse parameter because it relies on information given by the learners without any standardisation. To handle the dynamic and diffuse characteristic of prior knowledge, and to bridge the absence of a knowledge domain model, probabilistic techniques like latent semantic analysis are promising (van Bruggen et al. 2004). The absence of maintenance and structure in informal learning is also called the 'open corpus problem'. The open corpus problem applies when an unlimited set of documents is given that cannot be manually structured and indexed with domain concepts and metadata from a community (Brusilovsky and Henze 2007). The open corpus problem also applies to informal learning networks. Therefore, bottom-up recommendation techniques like collaborative filtering are more appropriate because they require nearly no maintenance and improve through the emergent behaviour of the community. Drachsler et al. (2008b) analysed how various types of collaborative filtering techniques can be used to support learners in informal learning networks. Following their conclusions we have to consider the different environmental conditions of informal learning, such as the lack of maintenance and less formal structured learning objects, in order to provide an appropriated navigation support to recommender systems. Learning networks are mainly structured by tags and ratings given by their users, being therefore in contrast with the institutionalised Learning Management Systems (LMSs) like Moodle (http://moodle.org) or Blackboard (http://www.blackboard.com) that are used to better manage learning activities and distribute learning resources to learners.

Besides the already mentioned differences for prior knowledge in informal learning, there are also differences in the data sets which are derived from environmental conditions. Normally, the numbers of ratings obtained in recommender systems is usually very small compared to the number of ratings that have to be predicted. Effective prediction by ratings based on small amounts is very essential for recommender systems and has an effect on the selection of a specific recommendation technique. Formal learning can rely on regular evaluations of experts or students upon multiple criteria (e.g. pedagogical quality, technical quality, ease of use) (Manouselis and Costopoulou 2007), but in informal learning environments such evaluation procedures are unstructured and few. Formal learning environments like universities often have integrated evaluation procedures for a regular quality evaluation to report to their funding body. With these integrated evaluation procedures more dense data sets can be expected. As a conclusion, the data sets in informal learning context are characterised by the 'Sparsity problem' caused by sparse ratings in the data set. Multi-criteria ratings could be beneficial for informal learning to overcome the 'Sparsity problem' of the data sets. These multi-criteria ratings have to be reasonable for the community of lifelong learners. The community could rate learning resources on various levels, such as required prior knowledge level (novice to expert), the presentation style of learning resources, and even the level of attractiveness, because keeping students satisfied and motivated is a vital criteria in informal learning. These explicit rating procedures should be supported with several indirect measures like 'Amount of learners using the learning resource' or 'Amount of adjustments of a learning resources', in order to measure how up-to-date the learning resource is.

Informal learning is therefore different from well-structured domains, like formal learning. Recommender systems for informal learning have no official maintenance by an institution, mostly rely on its community and most of the time do not contain well-defined metadata structures. Moreover, formal learning is characteristically top-down designed and the learning contents are a closed-corpus that can only be edited by domain experts; Informal learning contents emerge from the bottom-upwards through communities contributions (open-corpus) and every community member can adjust and contribute information. Therefore, it will be difficult to transfer and apply recommender systems even from formal to non-formal settings (and vice-versa), since user tasks and recommendation goals are often substantially different.

A critical assessment of recommender techniques regarding their applicability and usefulness in TEL has taken place by Drachsler et al. (2008a). Table 1.2 provides an initial overview of advantages and disadvantages of each technique, and reports the

Table 1.2 A selected list of recommendation technique used in TEL and their usefulness for learning

Name	Short description	Advantages	Disadvantages	Usefulness for TEL
Collaborative filtering (CF) techniques				
1. User-based CF	Users that rated the same item similarly probably have the same taste. Based on this assumption, this technique recommends unseen items already rated by similar users.	– No content analysis – Domain-independent – Quality improves over time – Bottom-up approach – Serendipity	– New user problem – New item problem – Popular taste – Scalability – Sparsity – Cold-start problem	– Benefits from experience –Allocates learners to groups (based on similar ratings)
2. Item-based CF	Focus on items, assuming that items rated similarly are probably similar. It recommends items with highest correlation (based on ratings to the items).	– No content analysis – Domain-independent – Quality improves over time – Bottom-up approach – Serendipity	– New item problem – Popular taste – Sparsity – Cold-start problem	– Benefits from experience
3. Stereotypes or demographics CF	Users with similar attributes are matched, then recommends items that are preferred by similar users (based on user data instead of ratings).	– No cold-start problem – Domain-independent –Serendipity	–Obtaining information –Insufficient information – Only popular taste –Obtaining metadata information –Maintenance ontology	–Allocates learners to groups –Benefits from experience –Recommendation from the beginning of the RS

(Continued)

Table 1.2 (continued)

Name	Short description	Advantages	Disadvantages	Usefulness for TEL
Content-based (CB) techniques				
4. Case-based reasoning	Assumes that if a user likes a certain item, s.lhe will probably also like similar items. Recommends new but similar items.	– No content analysis – Domain-independent – Quality improves over time	– New user problem – Overspecialisation – Sparsity – Cold-start problem	– Keeps learner informed about learning goal – Useful for hybrid RS
5. Attribute-based techniques	Recommends items based on the matching of their attributes to the user profile. Attributes could be weighted for their importance to the user.	– No cold-start problem – No new user I new item problem – Sensitive to changes of preferences – Can include non-item related features – Can map from user needs to items	– Does not learn – Only works with categories – Ontology modeling and maintenance is required – Overspecialisation	– Useful for hybrid RS – Recommendation from the beginning
Data-Mining (DM) techniques				
6. Decision Trees (C4.5,ID3)	A decision tree represents a set of classifications created from a set of rules. They start form a single classification and branch out based on classification rules mined from the data.	– Easy to understand – High representation power	– Overspecialisation in small datasets – Can become very broad	– Visualize differences of learners from the data – Alternative approach to expert driven ontologies

(Continued)

Table 1.2 (continued)

Name	Short description	Advantages	Disadvantages	Usefulness for TEL
7. K-Nearest Neighbor (Isodata, Forgy)	Does not build an explicit model instead exams the categories of the K-most similar data points. K-means is often used in TEL recommenders to compute similarity of vector-based approaches.	–Simple approach only two parameters to select –Robust to noise –High representation power	–Difficult to select distance function d –Irrelevant data needs to be removed –Slower than model-based recommendations	–Recommend similar peers, or contents to learners –Cluster learners in groups
8. Vector-based models (TF-IDF, Singular value decomposition, Matrix Factorisation)	Vector-based approaches characterise items and users as vectors of factors in a 3D space. A high correlation between an item and a user can be used as recommendation but also predictions can be created.	–Suitable for sparse datasets –Can take temporal differences into account –Can take various implicit information into account does not need explicit ratings	–Content depended (Items with same context but different terms are not matched) –User keywords have to match semantic space	–Useful to monitor and predict learner performance –Can adapt to increased knowledge level of learners –Can mark learning resources that are not popular anymore

Extended version based on initial table of Drachsler et al. (2008a) envisaged usefulness of each technique for TEL recommenders. Nevertheless, it aims to serve as an initial basis for such a discussion, since a more detailed and elaborate survey of all existing recommendation methods and techniques can take place in the future.

References

G. Adomavicius, A. Tuzhilin, Towards the next generation of recommender systems: a survey of the state-of-the-art and possible extensions. IEEE Trans. Knowl. Data Eng. **17**(6), 734–749 (2005)

L. Aroyo, R. Mizoguchi, C. Tzolov, OntoAIMS: ontological approach to courseware authoring. Paper presented at the international conference on computers in education (ICCE 2003), Hong Kong, China, 2003, 2–5 December 2003, p. 8.

R. Baker, K. Yacef, The state of educational data mining in 2009: a review and future visions. J. Educ. Data Min. **1**(1), 3–17 (2010)

R. Baker, Data Mining for Education, in International Encyclopedia of Education, 3rd edn, ed. by B. McGaw, P. Peterson, E. Baker, vol. 7 (Elsevier, Oxford, 2010) pp. 112–118

M. Baldoni, C. Baroglio, I. Brunkhorst, E. Marengo, V. Patti, Reasoning-based curriculum sequencing and validation: integration in a service-oriented architecture, in *Proceedings of the 2nd European Conference on Technology Enhanced Learning, LNCS 4753*, ed. by E. Duval, R. Klamma, M. Wolpers (Springer, Berlin, 2007), pp. 426–431

P. Baudisch, Dynamic Information Filtering. Ph.D. thesis, GMD Research Series, No 16, Darmstad Technical University, p. 188, 2001

N.J. Belkin, W.B. Croft, Information filtering and information retrieval: two sides of the same coin? Commun. ACM **35**(12), 29–38 (1992)

P. Brusilovsky, W. Nejdl, in Adaptive Hypermedia and Adaptive Web, ed. by M. Singh. Practical Handbook of Internet Computing (CRC Press LLC, Baton Rouge, 2004)

P. Brusilovsky, Methods and techniques of adaptive hypermedia. User Model. User-Adap. Inter. **6**(2–3), 87–129 (1996)

P. Brusilovsky, Adaptive hypermedia. User Model. User-Adap. Inter. **11**(1–2), 87–110 (2001)

P. Brusilovsky, N. Henze, Open corpus adaptive educational hypermedia, in The Adaptive Web: Methods and Strategies of Web Personalization, LNCS 4321, ed. by P. Brusilovsky, A. Kobsa, W. Nejdl (Springer, Berlin, 2007), p. 696

P. Brusilovsky, L. Pesin, M. Zyryanov, Towards an adaptive hypermedia component for an intelligent learning environment, in Human-Computer Interaction, LNCS, ed. by L.J. Bass, J. Gornostaev, C. Unger (Springer, Berlin, 1993), p. 358

R. Burke, Hybrid recommender systems: survey and experiments. User Model. User-Adap. Inter. **12**, 331–370 (2002)

R. Burke, Hybrid web recommender systems, in The Adaptive Web: Methods and Strategies of Web Personalization, LNCS, ed. by P. Brusilovsky, A. Kobsa, W. Neidl (Springer, Berlin, 2007), p. 408

R. Burke, M. Ramezani, in *Matching Recommendation Technologies and Domains*, ed. by F. Ricci, L. Rokach, B. Shapira, Recommender Systems Handbook (Springer, Berlin, 2011), pp. 367–386

A. Chervenak, I. Foster, C. Kesselman, C. Salisbury, S. Tuecke, The data grid: towards an architecture for the distributed management and analysis of large scientific data sets. J. Netw. Comput. Appl. **23**(3), 187–200 (2000)

A. Cristea, Authoring of adaptive hypermedia. Educ. Technol. Soc. **8**(3), 6–8 (2005)

P. De Bra, Teaching hypertext and hypermedia through the Web. J. Univ. Comput. Sci. **2**(12), 797–804 (1996)

P. De Bra, A. Aerts, D. Smits, N. Stash, AHA! version 2.0, more adaptation flexibility for authors. Paper presented at the world conference on e-Learning in corporate, goverment, healthcare and higher education, Montreal, Canada, 15–19 October 2002

B. De La Passardiere, A. Dufresne, Adaptive navigational tools for educational hypermedia, in *ICCAL'92, 4th International Conference on Computers and Learning*, ed. by I. Tomek (Springer, Berlin, 1992), pp. 555–567

M. Deshpande, G. Karypis, Item-based top-N recommendation algorithms. ACM Trans. Inf. Syst. 22(1), 143–177 (2004)

H. Drachsler, H. Hummel, R. Koper, Personal recommender systems for learners in lifelong learning: requirements, techniques and model. Int. J. Learn. Technol. 3(4), 404–423 (2008a)

H. Drachsler, H. Hummel, R. Koper, Using Simulations to Evaluate the Effects of Recommender Systems for Learners in Informal Learning Networks. ed. by R. Vuorikari, B. Kieslinger, R. Klamma, E. Duval, SIRTEL workshop at the 3rd EC-TEL conference. in Proceedings of the CEUR Workshop, Vol. 382, Maastricht, The Netherlands, 2008b

H. Drachsler, Navigation Support for Learners in Informal Learning Networks (2009a), Open University of the Netherlands. http://dspace.ou.nl/handle/1820/2084 Accessed 12 March 2012

H. Drachsler, H. Hummel, B. Van den Berg, J. Eshuis, A. Berlanga, R. Nadolski, W. Waterink, N. Boers, R. Koper, Effects of the ISIS recommender system for navigation support in self-organised learning networks. J. Educ. Technol. Soc. 12, 122–135 (2009b)

H. Drachsler, B. Hoisl, C. Wagenlecher, User-tailored inter-widget communication. Extending the shared data interface for the apache wookie engine. International conference on interactive computer aided learning 2010, Hasselt, Belgium, 2010a

H. Drachsler, T. Bogers, R. Vuorikari, K. Verbert, E. Duval, N. Manouselis, G. Beham, S. Lindstaedt, H. Stern, M. Friedrich, Issues and considerations regarding sharable data sets for recommender systems in technology enhanced learning. Procedia Comput. Sci. 1(2), 2849–2858 (2010b)

H. Drachsler, K. Verbert, M-A. Sicilia, M. Wolpers, N. Manouselis, R. Vuorikari, S. Lindstaedt, F. Fischer, dataTEL-Datasets for Technology Enhanced Learning. STELLAR ARV White Paper (2011), http://oa.stellarnet.eu/open-archive/browse?resource=6756_v1 Accessed 12 March 2012

H. Drachsler, K. Verbert, N. Manouselis, S. Lindstaedt, R. Vuorikari, M. Wolpers, Preface for data-TEL Special Issue on Datasets and Data Supported Learning in Technology-Enhanced Learning, ed. by H. Drachsler, K. Verbert, N. Manouselis, S. Lindstaedt, R. Vuorikari, M. Wolpers. International Journal of Technology Enhanced Learning (IJTEL), (to appear)

M.D. Ekstrand, J.T. Riedl, J.A. Konstan, Collaborative filtering recommender systems. Found. Trends Hum Comput. Interact. 4(2), 81–173 (2010)

D. Goldberg, D. Nichols, B.M. Oki, D. Terry, Using collaborative filtering to weave an information tapestry. Commun. ACM 35(12), 61–70 (1992)

K. Goldberg, T. Roeder, D. Gupta, C. Perkins, Eigentaste: a constant time collaborative filtering algorithm. Inf. Retrieval 4(2), 133–151 (2001)

M. Gonschorek, C. Herzog, Using hypertext for an adaptive helpsystem in an intelligent tutoring system, in *Proceedings of the 7th World Conference on Artificial Intelligence in Education*, ed. by J. Greer (AACE, Washington DC, 1995), p. 282

D. Gordon, *Ants at Work: How an Insect Society is Organized* (Free Press, New York, 1999)

U. Hanani, B. Shapira, P. Shoval, Information filtering: overview of issues, research and systems. User Model. User-Adap. Inter. 11, 203–259 (2001)

J.L. Herlocker, J.A. Konstan, L.G. Terveen, J.T. Riedl, Evaluating collaborative filtering recommender systems. ACM Trans. Inf. Syst. 22(1), 5–53 (2004)

H. Hohl, H.-D. Böcker, R. Gunzenhäuser, Hypadapter: an adaptive hypertext system for exploratory learning and programming. User Model. User-Adap. Inter. 6(2–3), 131–156 (1996)

L.-P. Hung, A personalized recommendation system based on product taxonomy for one-to-one marketing online. Expert Syst. Appl. 29, 383–392 (2005)

A. Jameson, *Systems That Adapt to Their Users: An Integrative Perspective* (Saarland University, Saarbröucken, 2001)

S. Johnson, *Emergence* (Scribner, New York, 2001)

P. Karampiperis, D. Sampson, Adaptive learning resources sequencing in educational hypermedia systems. Educ. Technol. Soc. **8**(4), 128–147 (2005)

J. Kay, R.J. Kummerfeld, An individualised course for the C programming language. in *Proceedings of Second International WWW Conference*, Chicago, USA, 17–20 October 1994

J.A. Konstan, Introduction to recommender systems: algorithms and evaluation. ACM Trans. Inf. Syst. **22**(1), 1–4 (2004)

R. Koper, C. Tattersall, New directions for lifelong learning using network technologies. Br. J. Educ. Technol. **35**(6), 689–700 (2004)

R. Koper, E. Rusman, P. Sloep, Effective learning networks. Lifelong Learn. Eur. **1**, 18–27 (2005)

M. Kravcik, M. Specht, R. Oppermann, Evaluation of WINDS authoring environment, in Adaptive Hypermedia and Adaptive Web-Based Systems, LNCS, ed. by P. De Bra, W. Nejdl (Springer, Berlin, 2004), p. 175

O. Liber, Colloquia-a conversation manager. Campus-Wide. Inf. Syst. **17**, 56–61 (2000)

O. Liber, M. Johnson, Personal learning environments. Interact. Learn. Environ. **16**, 1–2 (2008)

P. Lops, M. de Gemmis, G. Semeraro, in *Content-Based Recommender Systems: State of the Art and Trends*, ed. by F. Ricci, L. Rokach, B. Shapira, Recommender Systems Handbook (Springer, Berlin, 2011), pp. 73–105

T. Malone, K. Grant, F. Turbak, S. Brobst, M. Cohen, Intelligent information sharing systems. Commun. ACM **30**(5), 390–402 (1987)

N. Manouselis, C. Costopoulou, Analysis and Classification of Multi-Criteria Recommender Systems. World Wide Web: Internet and Web Information Systems, Special Issue on Multi-channel Adaptive Information Systems on the World Wide Web **10**(4), 415–441 (2007)

N. Manouselis, H. Drachsler, K. Verbert, OC. Santos (eds.), in *Proceedings of the 1st Workshop on Recommender Systems for Technology Enhanced Learning (RecSysTEL 2010)*, Procedia Computer Science, vol. 1, no. 2

N. Manouselis, H. Drachsler, R. Vuorikari, H. Hummel, R. Koper, in Recommender Systems, in *Technology Enhanced Learning*, ed. by P. Kantor, F. Ricci, L. Rokach, B. Shapira (Recommender Systems Handbook (Springer, Berlin, 2011), pp. 387–415

N. Manouselis, R. Vuorikari, F. Van Assche, Simulated Analysis of MAUT Collaborative Filtering for Learning Object Recommendation. in *Proceedings of the Workshop on Social Information Retrieval in Technology Enhanced Learning (SIRTEL 2007)*, Crete, Greece, 2007

J.D. Moore, W.R. Swartout, *Pointing: a way toward explanation dialogue* (Eight National Conference on Artificial Intelligence, AAAI, 1990), pp. 457–464

X. Ochoa, Modeling the macro-behavior of learning object repositories. Interdisc. J. E-Learn. Learn. Objects **7**, 25–35 (2011)

R. Oppermann, Adaptively supported adaptability. Int. J. Hum. Comput. Stud. **40**(3), 455–472 (1994)

C. Paris, Tailoring object description to a user's level of expertise. Comput. Linguis. **14**(3), 64–78 (1988)

M. Pazzani, D. Billsus, Learning and revising user profiles: the identification of interesting web sites. Mach. Learn. **27**, 313–331 (1997)

D.M. Pennock, E. Horvitz, *Analysis of the axiomatic foundations of collaborative filtering, in Proceedings of the AAAI Workshop on Artificial Intelligence for Electronic Commerce* (Orlando, Florida, July, 1999)

T. Prez, J. Gutirrez, P. Lopistguy, An adaptive hypermedia system, in *Proceedings of the 7th World Conference on Artificial Intelligence in Education*, ed. by J. Greer (AACE, Washington DC, 1995), p. 358

W. Reinhardt, C. Meier, H. Drachsler, P. Sloep, Analyzing 5 years of EC-TEL Proceedings. ed. by C.D. Kloos, D. Gillet, R. Garca, F. Wild, M. Wolpers. in *Towards Ubiquitous Learning Proceedings of the 6th European Conference on Technology Enhanced Learning*, 2011a

W. Reinhardt, A. Wilke, M. Moi, H. Drachsler, P. Sloep, in *Mining and visualizing Research Networks using the Artefact-Actor-Network approach Learning*, ed. by A. Abraham (Springer, London, 2011b), pp. 1–34

P. Resnick, N. Iacovou, M. Suchak, P. Bergstrom, J. Riedl, GroupLens: an open architecture for collaborative filtering. in *Proceedings of ACM CSCW'94*, pp. 175–186, 1994

P. Resnick, H.R. Varian, Recommender systems. Commun. ACM **40**(3), 56–58 (1997)

C. Romero, S. Ventura, Educational data mining: a survey from 1995 to 2005. Expert Syst. Appl. **33**(1), 135–146 (2007)

C. Romero, S. Ventura, Educational data mining: a review of the state-of-the-art. IEEE Trans. Syst. Man Cybern. Part C Appl. Rev. **40**(6), 601–618 (2010)

C. Romero, S. Ventura, E. Garcia, Data mining in course management systems: MOODLE case study and tutorial. Comput. Educ. **51**(1), 368–384 (2008)

O.C. Santos, J.G. Boticario (eds.), Recommender Systems to Support the Dynamics of Virtual Learning Communities. in *International Journal of Web Based Communities (IJWBC)*, Inderscience (in press)

O.C. Santos, J.G. Boticario (eds.), *in Educational Recommender Systems and Technologies: Practices and Challenges* (IGI Global, Spain, 2012)

J.B. Schafer, D. Frankowski, J. Herlocker, S. Sen, Collaborative filtering systems, in *The Adaptive Web: Methods and Strategies of Web Personalization, Lecture Notes in Computer Science*, ed. by P. Brusilovsky, A. Kobsa, W. Neidl (Springer, Berlin, 2007), p. 324

J.B. Schafer, J.A. Konstan, J. Riedl, E-Commerce recommendation applications. Data Min. Knowl. Disc. **5**, 115–153 (2001)

A.I. Schein, A. Popescul, L. Ungar, D.M. Pennock, CROC: a new evaluation criterion for recommender systems. Electron. Commer. Res. **5**, 51–74 (2005)

M. Schneider-Hufschmidt, T. Kuhme, U. Malinowski (eds.), *Adaptive user interfaces: Principles and practice, Human Factors in Information Technology* (North-Holland, Amsterdam, 1993)

U. Shardanand, P. Maes, Social information filtering: algorithms for automatic 'word of mouth'. in *Proceedings of the Conference on Human Factors in Computing Systems (CHI'95)*, Denver CO, USA, 1995

G. Siemens, What are Learning Analytics? (2010), Retrieved 11 March 2012 http://www.elearnspace.org/blog/2010/08/25/what-are-learning-analytics/

G. Siemens, D. Gasevic (eds.), in *Proceedings of the 1st conference on Learning Analytics and Knowledge*, Banff, Calgary (ACM, Canada, 2011)

B. Smyth, Case-based recommendation, in *The Adaptive Web: Methods and Strategies of Web Personalization, Lecture Notes in Computer Science*, ed. by P. Brusilovsky, A. Kobsa, W. Neidl (Springer, Berlin, 2007), p. 376

T.Y. Tang, B.K. Daniel, C. Romero (eds.), Recommender systems for and in social and online learning environments. Expert Syst. J. Knowl. Eng. (to appear)

J. van Bruggen, P. Sloep, P. van Rosmalen, F. Brouns, H. Vogten, R. Koper, C. Tattersall, Latent semantic analysis as a tool for learner positioning in learning networks for lifelong learning. Br. J. Educ. Technol. **35**(6), 729–738 (2004)

K. Verbert, E. Duval, S.N. Lindstaedt, D. Gillet (eds.), Context-aware recommender systems. J. Univ. Comput. Sci. vol. 16, no. 16, pp. 2175–2178 (2010)

R. Vuorikari, R. Koper, Ecology of social search for learning resources. Campus-Wide Inf. Syst. **26**(4), 272–286 (2009)

R. Vuorikari, N. Manouselis, E. Duval (eds.), Special issue on social information retrieval for technology enhanced learning. J. Digit. Inf. vol. 10, no. 2, (2009)

M. Waldrop, *Complexity: The Emerging Science at the Edge of Chaos* (Simon and Schuster, New York, 1992)

S. Weibelzahl, *PhD Dissertation, Evaluation of Adaptive Systems* (University of Trier, Germany, 2003)

F. Wild, F. Moedritscher, S.E. Sigurdarson, Designing for change: mash-up personal learning environments. eLearn. Papers. **9**, (2008)

S. Wilson, P. Sharples, D. Griffith, Distributing education services to personal and institutional systems using Widgets. ed. by F. Wild, M. Kalz, M. Palmer (eds.), Mash-Up Personal Learning Environments, in *Proceedings of the 1st MUPPLE workshop, CEUR-Proceedings*, vol. 388, Maastricht, 2008

Chapter 2
TEL as a Recommendation Context

Abstract In this chapter, we define the TEL recommendation problem and identify TEL recommendation goals. More specifically, we reflect on user tasks that are supported in TEL settings, and how they compare to typical user tasks in other recommender systems. Then, we present an analysis of existing data sets that capture contextual learner interactions with tools and resources in TEL settings. These data sets can be used for a wide variety of research purposes, including experimental comparison of the performance of recommendation algorithms for learning.

2.1 TEL Recommendation

2.1.1 Defining the TEL Recommendation Problem

In a recommender system, the items of interest and the user preferences are represented in various forms, e.g. using a single or multiple attributes for describing an item. Particularly in systems where recommendations are based on the opinion of others, it is crucial to take into consideration the multiple factors or criteria that affect the users' opinions in order to make more effective recommendations. In related research, the problem of recommendation has been identified as the way to help individuals in a community to find the information or products that are most likely to be interesting to them or to be relevant to their needs (Konstan 2004). It has been further refined to the problem (i) of predicting whether a particular user will like a particular item (prediction problem), or (ii) of identifying a set of N items that will be of interest to a certain user (top-N recommendation problem) (Adomavicius and Tuzhilin 2005). Therefore, the general recommendation problem can be formulated as follows (Deshpande and Karypis 2004): let C be the set of all users and S the set of all possible items that can be recommended. We define as $U^c(S)$ a utility function $U^c(S) : C \times S \rightarrow \Re^+$ that measures the appropriateness of recommending an item s to user c. It is assumed that this function is not known for the whole $C \times S$ space

N. Manouselis et al., *Recommender Systems for Learning*,
SpringerBriefs in Electrical and Computer Engineering,
DOI: 10.1007/978-1-4614-4361-2_2, © The Authors 2013

but only on some subset of it. Therefore, in the context of recommendation, we want for each user $c \in C$ to be able to:

i   estimate (or approach) the utility function $U^c(S)$ for an item s of the space S for which $U^c(S)$ is not yet known; or,

ii choose a set of N items $s \in S$ that will maximise $U^c(S)$: $\forall c \in C$, $s = argmax_{s \in S} U^c$

In most recommender systems, the utility function $U^c(S)$ usually considers one attribute of an item, e.g. its overall evaluation or rating. Nevertheless, utility may also involve more than one attribute of an item. The recommendation problem therefore becomes a multi-attribute one. We want to explore how the TEL recommendation problem can be better defined if such a multi-attribute modelling approach is followed in order to identify (Roy 1996):

- *Object of the decision*. That is, defining the object upon which the decision has to be made and the rationale of the recommendation decision.
- *Family of criteria*. That is, the identification and modelling of a set of criteria that affect the recommendation decision, and which are exhaustive and non-redundant.
- *Global preference model*. That is, the definition of the function that aggregates the marginal preferences upon each criterion into the global preference of the decision maker about each item.
- *Decision support process*. That is, the study of the various categories and types of recommender systems that may be used to support the recommendation decision maker, in accordance to the results of the previous steps.

In TEL recommendation, the object of decision is an item s that belongs to the set of all candidate items S representing any type of items that may be recommended to a user, such as a learning resource, a learning activity, a peer learner or a mentor. To express the rationale behind the decision, Roy (1996) refers to the notion of the decision *problematic*. The four types of common decision problematics identified in the Multi-Criteria Decision Making (MCDM) literature, may be considered valid in the context of TEL recommendation (Adomavicius et al. 2011):

- *Choice*, which involves choosing one item from a set of candidates;
- *Sorting*, which involves classifying items into pre-defined categories;
- *Ranking*, which involves ranking items from the best one to the worst one; and
- *Description*, which involves describing all the items in terms of performance upon each criterion.

For instance, in TEL contexts, a set of candidates may be learning resources, peer learners or learning activities. An example family of criteria that affects the recommendation decision can include the age, language, knowledge level, goal or other contextual variables such as the current device and available time of the learner. *Choice* involves choosing those objects that are appropriate for the learning setting and characteristics of the learner—such as learning resources to study the theory of relativity for K-12 learners in French. A TEL recommender system that supports *sorting* classifies items into predefined categories—in its simplest form such sorting may constitute classifying items according to certain attributes, such as language or knowledge level. *Ranking* is the process of presenting items according to descending order of relevance. For instance, in a TEL context, such ranking may involve presenting those items that are most relevant for the age, knowledge level or mother tongue of the learner first. Finally, *description* involves presenting and explaining each one of the candidate items by analysing its predicted performance upon each one of the criteria. Such a description enables the user to gain insight into the various alternatives and help her take better informed decisions.

After the correct problematic is defined, the set of all candidate items S is analysed in terms of multiple criteria, in order to model all possible impacts, consequences, or attributes (Roy 1996). In recommender systems, the criteria may refer to multiple characteristics of an item (usually the case in content-based recommendation) or to the multiple dimensions upon which the item is being evaluated (the case in collaborative filtering recommendation). This step must conclude to a consistent family of n criteria $\{g_1, g_2, \ldots, g_n\}$. In MCDM, four types of criteria are formally used (Jacquet-Lagreze and Siskos 2001):

- *Measurable*, is a criterion that allows quantified measurement upon an evaluation scale.
- *Ordinal*, is a criterion that defines an ordered set in the form of a qualitative or a descriptive scale.
- *Probabilistic*, is a criterion that uses probability distributions to cover uncertainty in the evaluation of alternatives.
- *Fuzzy*, is a criterion where evaluation of alternatives is represented in relationship to its possibility to belong in one of the intervals of the evaluation scale.

For instance, a measurable criterion that is used by a content-based recommender can be the age range of learners for which a learning resource is suitable. Examples of ordinal criteria are attributes that belong to an ordered controlled vocabulary, like the aggregation level of a resource and its easiness to understand. Probabilistic and fuzzy criteria are often used when a system has to deal with uncertainty of a criterion—such as an estimate of the knowledge level of the user or an estimate of the usefulness of a resource for a particular learning activity.

After the definition of the criteria, the development of a global preference model is made to provide a way to aggregate the values of each criterion g_i (with $i = 1, \ldots, n$) in order to express the preferences between the different alternatives of the item set S. Examples of preference models include (Adomavicius et al. 2011):

- *Value-Focused models*, where a value system for aggregating the user preferences on the different criteria is constructed. In such approaches, marginal preferences upon each criterion are synthesised into a total value using a synthesising utility function (Keeney 1992).
- *Outranking Relations models*, where preferences are expressed as a system of outranking relations between two alternatives a and b, thus allowing the expression of incomparability. In such approaches, all alternatives are one-to-one compared between them, and preference relations are provided as relations *a is preferred*

to b, a is equally preferred to b, and *a is incomparable to b* (Roy and Bouyssou 1993).

- *Multi-Objective Optimisation models*, where criteria are expressed in the form of multiple constraints of a multi-objective optimisation problem. In such approaches, usually the goal is to find a Pareto optimal solution for the original optimisation problem (Zeleny 1974).
- *Preference Disaggregation models*, where the preference model is derived by analysing past decisions. Such approaches build on the models proposed by the previous ones (thus they are sometimes considered as a sub-category of other modelling approaches' categories), since they try to infer a preference model of a given form (e.g. value function) from some given preferential structures that have led to particular decisions in the past, and aim at producing decisions that are at least identical to the examined past ones (Jacquet-Lagreze and Siskos 2001).

The most typical cases of TEL recommender systems are value-focused (Manouselis et al. 2011), usually engaging a single-attribute (and rarely multi-attribute), linear, additive value function for the representation of user preferences. This is a traditional decision making approach, widely applied and convenient to implement. On the other hand, assuming that the preference function is single-attribute and linear restricts the way user preferences are represented. Therefore, alternative forms for representing preferences in a MCDM manner should be explored in TEL as well (Manouselis 2008; Adomavicius et al. 2011). This requirement is particularly relevant for TEL, where certain attributes may have a different influence on recommendation in different settings. For instance, both formal and informal learning processes have different requirements for the learning environment and, as such, for the recommendation within the environment. Often, it is not possible to draw a clear line between formal and informal learning scenarios. As an example, recommender systems need to deal with the tension of recommendations for activities liked by the learner and those required by the teacher (Tang and McCalla 2003). Since recommendations may differ depending on the context of the learner, it is therefore important to study carefully the intended recommendation goals to be supported. We identify such goals in the next section.

2.1.2 Identifying the TEL Recommendation Goals

In the past, the development of recommender systems has been related to a number of relevant user tasks that the recommender system supports within some particular application context. More specifically, Herlocker et al. (2004) have related popular (or less popular) user tasks with a number of specific recommendation goals that are included in Table 2.1. Generally speaking, most of these already identified recommendation goals and user tasks are valid in the case of TEL recommender systems as well. For example, a recommender system supporting learners to achieve a specific learning goal, providing annotation in context or recommending a sequence of learning resources are relevant tasks. In the table, an example of how recommendation could support a similar user task is included for all the tasks that Herlocker et al. (2004) have identified. In addition, it includes a comment about any additional requirements that this brings forward for the developers of TEL recommender systems.

On the other hand, in comparison to the typical item recommendation scenario, there are several particularities to be considered regarding what kind of learning is desired, e.g. learning a new concept or reinforce existing knowledge may require different types of learning resources. This is reflected in the second part of Table 2.1, where examples of user tasks that are particularly interesting for TEL are in, extending the ones initially identified in Manouselis et al. (2011). Again, a comment on any additional requirements for developers of TEL recommenders is included.

Apart from this initial identification of tasks, recommendation in a TEL context has many particularities that are based on the richness of the pedagogical theories and models. For instance, for learners with no prior knowledge in a specific domain, relevant pedagogical rules such as Vygotsky's *zone of proximal development* could be applied: e.g. 'recommended learning objects should have a level slightly above learners' current competence level' (Vygotsky 1978). Different from buying products, learning is an effort that often takes more time and interactions compared to a commercial transaction. Learners rarely achieve a final end state after a fixed time. Instead of buying a product and then owning it, learners achieve different levels of competences that have various levels in different domains. In such scenarios, what is important is identifying the relevant learning goals and supporting learners in achieving them. On the other hand, depending on the context, some particular user task may be prioritised. This could call for recommendations whose time span is longer than the one of product recommendations, or recommendations of similar learning resources, since recapitulation and reiteration are central tasks of the learning process (McCalla 2004).

As for teacher-centered learning contexts, different tasks need to be supported. These tasks cover both the ones related to the preparation of lessons, the delivery of a lesson (i.e. the actual teaching), and the ones related to the evaluation/assessment. For instance, to prepare a lesson the teacher has certain educational goals to fulfill and needs to match the delivery methods to the profile of the learners (e.g. their previous knowledge). Lesson preparation can include a variety of information seeking tasks, such as finding content to motivate the learners, to recall existing knowledge, to illustrate, visualise and represent new concepts and information. The delivery can be supported in using different pedagogical methods (either supported with TEL or not), whose effectiveness is evaluated according to the goals set. A TEL recommender system could support one or more of these tasks, leading to a variety of recommendation goals.

Thus, although the previously identified user tasks and recommendation goals can be considered valid in a TEL context, there are several particularities and complexities. This means that simply transferring a recommender system from an existing (e.g. commercial) content to TEL may not accurately meet the needs of the targeted users. In TEL, careful analysis of the targeted users and their supported tasks should

Table 2.1 User tasks supported by current recommender systems and requirements for TEL recommender systems

Tasks	Description	Generic recommender	TEL recommenders	New requirements
Existing user tasks supported by recommender systems				
1. ANNOTATION IN CONTEXT	Recommendations while user carries out other tasks	E.g. predicting how relevant the links are within a web page	E.g. predicting relevance/usefulness of items in the reading list of a Moodle course or a Learning Network	Explore attributes for representing relevance/usefulness in a learning context
2. FIND GOOD ITEMS	Recommendations of suggested items	E.g. receiving list of web pages to visit	E.g. receiving a selected list of online educational resources around a topic	None
3. FIND ALL GOOD ITEMS	Recommendation of all relevant items	E.g. receiving a complete list of references on a topic	E.g. suggesting a complete list of scientific literature or blog postings around a topic	None
4. RECOMMEND SEQUENCE	Recommendation of a sequence of items	E.g. receive a proposed sequence of songs	E.g. receiving a proposed sequence through resources to achieve a particular learning goal	Explore formal and informal attributes for representing relevancy to a particular learning goal
5. JUST BROWSING	Recommendations out of the box while user is browsing	E.g. people that bought this, have also bought that	E.g. receiving recommendations for new courses on the university site or getting suggestions for additional blog postings in a Learning Network	Explore formal and informal attributes for representing relevance/usefulness in a learning context
6. FIND CREDIBLE RECOMMENDER	Recommendations during initial exploration/testing phase of a system	E.g. movies that you will definitely like	E.g. restricting initial recommendations to ones with high confidence /credibility	Explore criteria for measuring confidence and credibility in formal and informal learning

(Continued)

Table 2.1 (continued)

Tasks	Description	Generic recommender	TEL recommenders	New requirements
TEL user tasks that could be supported by recommender systems				
1. FIND NOVEL RESOURCES	Recommendations of particularly new or novel items	E.g. receiving recommendations about latest additions or particularly controversial items	E.g. receiving very new and/or controversial resources on covered topics	Explore recommendation techniques that select items beyond their similarity
2. FIND PEERS	Recommendation of other people with relevant interests	E.g. being suggested profiles of users with similar interests	E.g. being suggested student in the same class or a peer-student in a Learning Network	Explore attributes for measuring the similarity with other people
3. FIND GOOD PATHWAYS	Recommendation of alternative learning paths through learning resources	E.g. receive alternative sequences of similar songs	E.g. receiving a list of alternative learning paths over the same resources to achieve a learning goal depending	Explore criteria for the construction and suggestion of alternative (but similar) sequences
4. PREDICT STUDENT PERFORMANCE	Prediction of student performance based on previous behavior	E.g. predicting student performance in visual graphs compared to average student scores	E.g. recommending group combinations for teachers to improve course performance, recommending learning activities to improve individual student performance	Take advantage of student data from LMS, tracking of students and teacher activities, critical interpretation of analysed data

be carried out, before a recommendation goal is defined and a recommender system is deployed. This means that the TEL recommendation goals can be rather complex: for example, a typical TEL recommender system could suggest a number of alternative learning paths throughout a variety of learning resources, either in the form of learning sequences or hierarchies of interacting learning resources. This should take place in a pedagogically meaningful way that will reflect the individual learning goals and targeted competence levels of the user, depending on proficiency levels, specific interests and the intended application context. A number of context variables have to be considered, such as user attributes, domain characteristics, and intelligent methods that can be engaged to provide personalised recommendations.

2.1.3 Identifying the TEL Context Variables

As outlined by Romero and Ventura (2007), the TEL domain differs from domains like e-commerce in several ways. In e-commerce, the used data are often simple web server access logs or ratings of users on items. In TEL, many researchers use more information about a learner interaction (Pahl and Donnellan 2002). The user model and the objectives of the systems are also different in both application domains (Drachsler et al. 2009a).

A survey of existing TEL interaction data models has been presented in Butoianu et al. (2010). Examples of models to represent learner interactions are the User Interaction Context Ontology (UICO, Rath et al. 2009) and Contextualised Attention Metadata (CAM, Scheffel et al. 2011) models. Both models capture actions of the user, such as *select*, *save*, *create* and *write* actions, on resources. In addition, the context in which an action occurred, such as the current task of the learner, can be captured. The Atom activity stream Resource Description Framework (RDF) mapping of the LinkedEducation.org initiative presents a similar approach to model actions of users in social networks. Vocabularies for actions, actors and objects involved and related contextual information are defined.

In addition to interaction models, researchers in TEL have elaborated learner models that describe several characteristics of learners. Brusilovsky and Millan (2007) identified the following categories based on an analysis of the existing literature: *knowledge levels, goals and tasks, interests, background* and *learning and cognitive styles*. In addition, several models, standards and specifications have been elaborated to describe learning resources. The IEEE LOM and Dublin Core metadata standards are prominently used by TEL applications to describe characteristics of learning resources, including general characteristics, such as title, author and keywords, technical and educational characteristics and relations between learning resources.

We integrated the various data categories and elements in Fig. 2.1. We use this framework in the remainder of this chapter to identify data elements in existing data sets. The model has been developed by synthesising existing works on interaction data and context variables in the TEL field that were outlined above. It could be further refined by studying relevant theoretical frameworks, like the Activity

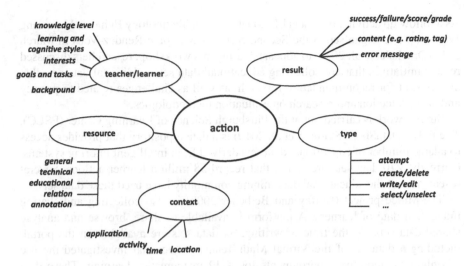

Fig. 2.1 TEL variables (adapted from Verbert et al. (to appear)

Theory (Kaptelinin et al. 1995), that could help reorganise the various categories and elements.

2.2 Data Sets to Support TEL Recommendation

2.2.1 Collecting TEL Data Sets

An important requirement to facilitate research on recommendation technologies is the existence of sufficient data from various system activities and its interactions with users. When the analysis is taking place for research purposes and in an exploratory manner, it is equally important to provide researchers with sufficient data coming from a real or simulated environment of the targeted domain. In an increasing number of scientific disciplines, large data collections are emerging as important community resources (Chervenak et al. 2000). These data sets are used as benchmarks to develop new algorithms and compare them to other algorithms in given settings. In data sets that are used for recommendations algorithms, such data can for instance be explicit (ratings) or implicit (downloads and tags) relevance indicators. These indicators are then for instance used to find users with similar interests as a basis to suggest items to a user.

To collect TEL data sets, the first dataTEL Challenge was launched as part of the Workshop on Recommender Systems for TEL (Manouselis et al. 2010a), jointly organised by the 4th ACM Conference on Recommender Systems and the 5th European Conference on Technology Enhanced Learning in September 2010. In this call, research groups were invited to submit existing data sets from TEL applications.

As a follow up activity, the dataTEL—Data sets for Technology Enhanced Learning Workshop was organised at the Second STELLAR Alpine Rendez-Vous in March 2011 (Drachsler et al. 2011, to appear). During this workshop, researchers discussed related initiatives that are collecting educational data sets, additional data sets that are relevant for recommendation research, as well as challenges related to privacy and data protection and research on evaluation methodologies.

Similar work is carried out at the Pittsburgh Science of Learning Center (PSLC). The PSLC DataShop (Stamper et al. 2010) is a data repository that provides access to a large number of educational data sets derived from intelligent tutoring systems. Currently, 270 data sets are stored that record 58 million learner actions. Several researchers of the educational data mining community have used these data sets.

The Mulce project (Reffay and Betbeder 2009) is also collecting and sharing interaction data of learners. A platform is available to share, browse and analyse shared data sets. At the time of writing, 34 data sets are available on the portal, including a data set of the Virtual Math Teams project that investigated the use of online collaborative environments for K-12 mathematics learning. These data sets have been used extensively by the Computer Supported Collaborative Learning (CSCL) community.

LinkedEducation.org is another initiative that provides an open platform to promote the use of data for educational purposes. Available data sets describe the structure of organisations and institutions, the structure of courses, learning resources and interrelationships between people. Schemas and vocabularies are provided to describe discourse relationships and activity streams. Such schemas and vocabularies offer interesting perspectives for the sharing and reuse of interaction data between users that is relevant for research on recommendation techniques.

Several other initiatives are available that focus on providing the means to share data sets among researchers in a more generic way. DataCite.org is an organisation that enables users to register research data sets and to assign persistent identifiers to them, so that data sets can be handled as citable scientific objects. The Dataverse Network (King 2007) is an open-source application for publishing, citing and discovering research data. Fact sheets of data sets are gathered from organisations and researchers are encouraged to make data publicly available.

In this section, we analyse educational data sets that have been collected by dataTEL (Drachsler et al. 2010a) and that can be used for research on recommendation for learning. A detailed description of other data sets and their usefulness for a wider variety of research purposes may be found at Verbert et al. (2011) and Verbert et al. (to appear).

2.2.2 Collected Data Sets

Table 2.2 presents the data sets have been collected as a result of the first dataTEL challenge:

Table 2.2 Overview data sets

	Mendeley	APOSDLE	ReMashed	Organic Edunet	Mace	Travel well	CGIAR
Collection period	1 year	3 months	2 years	9 months	3 years	6 months	6 years
Number of users	200.000	6	140	1.000	1.148	98	841
Number of items	1.857.912	163	96.000	10.500	12.000	1.923	14.693
Number of actions	4.848.725	1.500	23.264	920	461.982	16.353	326.339
Publicly available	+	+	–	–	–	+	–
Action							
Attempt	–	–	–	–	–	–	+
Select/unselect	+	+	+	–	+	–	+
Tags	–	+	+	+	+	+	–
Rate/star	+	–	–	+	+	+	–
Save/download	+	+	–	–	–	–	–
Search	–	+	+	–	–	–	–
Learner/teacher							
Id	+	+	+	+	+	+	+
Knowledge level	–	+	+	–	–	–	–
Interests	–	+	+	–	+	+	+
Resource							
General	+	+	+	+	+	+	+
Technical	–	–	–	–	+	+	–
Educational	–	–	–	+	+	+	–
Annotation	–	–	+	–	–	–	–
Context							
Time	–	+	+	+	+	+	+
Activity	–	+	–	–	–	–	–
Result							
Success/failure	–	+	–	–	–	–	+
Content (e.g. rating, tag)	–	–	+	+	+	+	+

- The first data set was submitted by *Mendeley* (Jack et al. to appear), a research platform that helps users organise research papers and collaborate with colleagues. In the context of learning, such a data set provides useful data for recommender systems that suggest papers to learners or teachers or to suggest suitable peer learners on the basis of common research or learning interests. The data set contains *learner* and *resource* data. For each learner, implicit interest data is available that captures which papers a user has selected, starred or added to her library.

- The *APOSDLE* data set originates from the APOSDLE (Ghidini et al. 2007) project. APOSDLE is an adaptive learning system that aims to support learning within everyday work tasks. The system recommends resources (documents, videos, links) and colleagues who can help a user with a task. The data set captures information about the *activity context* (tasks, topics), the *learner* (knowledge level, implicit interest indicators) and actions on *resources*.

- The *ReMashed* data set focuses on community knowledge sharing (Drachsler et al. 2010b). The data set includes information about interests of *learners* (ratings and tags) on available *resources*. The main objective of ReMashed is to offer personalized information access to the emergent information space of the community.

- The *MACE* data set originates from the MACE *eContentplus* project (Wolpers et al. 2009). The MACE portal provides advanced graphical metadata based access to learning resources in architecture that are stored in different repositories all over Europe. The data set contains both implicit (search activities, select, downloads, tags) and explicit (ratings) interest data of the *learner* on *resources*. In addition, the *time* of each user activity is recorded.

- The *Organic.Edunet* data set was collected on the Organic.Edunet Web portal (Manouselis et al. 2009), a learning portal for organic agriculture educators that provides access a large number of learning resources from a federation of 11 institutional repositories. The data set includes *learner* (interest data in the form of tags and ratings) and *resource* data. The particularity of this data set is the fact that ratings are collected upon three different criteria: the usefulness of a resource as a learning tool, the relevance to the organic thematic, and the quality of its metadata.

- The *Travel well* data set originates from the MELT *eContentplus* project (Vuorikari 2009). The data set was collected on the MELT Learning Resource Exchange portal that makes open educational resources available from 20 content providers in Europe and elsewhere. This data set includes information about *teachers* (interest indicators in the form of tags and ratings and topics of interests as provided by the teachers), *resources* (minimum age, maximum age, duration, resource type, duration) and the *timestamp* of user actions.

- The *CGIAR* contains data from a Moodle installation used for agroforestry courses of CGIAR[1]—a worldwide network of Agricultural Research Centers. The data set contains actions of learners on quizzes and retrieval of documents provided by the teacher through a Moodle LMS.

---

[1] http://cgiar.org

The CGIAR, MACE, Organic.Edunet and Mendeley data sets are the largest data sets that contain data of 841, 1.148, 1000 and 200.000 users during a time period of 6 years, 3 years, 9 months and 1 years, respectively. The Travel well data set contains ratings and tags of about 100 users that were collected during a six month time period. The ReMashed data sets collects activities of 140 users during a 2 year period. The current APOSDLE data set is only a sample that captures data of a few users only.

Several data sets have been collected that are openly accessible. Registration is sometimes required before a dataset can be downloaded. For other datasets, legal protection rules apply. We obtained these data sets by sending a statement of our intended research purposes to the organisation. These statements were then in most cases analysed by their legal department before approval was granted. All data sets contain data that is anonymised, so that it can no longer be linked to an individual.

2.2.3 Usefulness for TEL Recommender Systems

Several dataTEL data sets contain relevance indicators that are useful for research on recommendation algorithms for learning. Of interest in this discussion are the data elements that are provided by the data sets. Explicit relevance feedback, such as ratings by users, are provided in the MACE, ReMashed, Organic.Edunet and Travel well data sets. These data sets provide ratings on a five point likert scale and are interesting data sets for developing recommendation algorithms to *find novel resources*. Mendeley provides information on articles that are starred by a user ('1' if the article has been starred and '0' otherwise), but the semantics of such stars in user libraries may be different for different users (i.e. a star can indicate relevance feedback, but may as well indicate that the user wants to read the article at a later stage). Therefore, the application of such data for recommendation is less straightforward. In addition, implicit relevance indicators, such as downloads, search terms and annotations, are available. If time interval data is available, the data might be suitable to extract reading times in order to determine the relevancy of a resource.

Manouselis et al. (2007, 2010b) used the Travel well data set to evaluate recommendation algorithms for learning. Similar experiments have been reported in Verbert et al. (2011). In this study, the Mendeley and MACE data sets were also used. Although still preliminary, some conclusions were drawn about successful parameterisation of collaborative filtering algorithms for learning. Outcomes suggest that the use of implicit relevance indicators, such as downloads, tags and read actions, are useful to suggest learning resources.

The data sets can also be used for research to *find peers*. For instance, by analysing interaction patterns of learners, a recommender system may identify peer helpers who are able to help with a learning activity. In addition, data sets derived from web portals, such as the Organic.Edunet, MACE, Mendeley, and Travel well data sets, can be used for finding users with common interests. Such prediction of user attributes has been researched extensively by the Educational Data Mining community and includes finding estimates of the knowledge level of a user based on interaction data.

An extensive overview of research in this area has been presented in Romero and Ventura (2007).

Finding good pathways is a third recommendation task that is relevant for a TEL context. There are several ways to support research on recommendation of such learning sequences. Time information can be used to extract sequencing patterns from data sets that capture interactions of users with resources, such as select, annotate, rate or download actions. Such information is available in many dataTEL data sets, including the ReMashed, MACE, Organic.Edunet, Travel well and CGIAR data sets. Drachsler et al. (2009b) researched the influence of sequence recommendation on the learning process with the ReMashed data set. An alternative way to support sequence recommendation would be to find pathways based on other learner characteristics, such as knowledge level. Such research has been conducted by the Intelligent Tutoring Systems community. Cheung et al. (2003) for instance suggest next learning resources that relate to prior knowledge of the course in order to provide good "orientation", which is the pathway to learn the material.

Predicting student performance is a fourth recommendation task that has been researched extensively over the last decade. Several data sets are available that can support research on prediction of learner performance and discovery of learner models. Among others, such predictions are researched to provide advice when a learner is solving a problem (Romero and Ventura 2007). Data sets from intelligent tutoring systems that capture attempts of learners provide a rich source of data to estimate the knowledge level of a learner. Some data sets derived from LMSs, such as the CGIAR data set, contain data on the number of attempts and total time spent on assignments, forums and quizzes. Romero et al. (2008) compared different data mining techniques to classify learners based on such LMS data and the final grade obtained for courses. A more extensive analysis of usefulness of data sets for learning analytics purposes has been presented in Verbert et al. (to appear).

References

G. Adomavicius, A. Tuzhilin, Towards the next generation of recommender systems: a survey of the state-of-the-art and possible extensions. IEEE Trans. Knowl. Data Eng. **17**(6), 734–749 (2005)

G. Adomavicius, N. Manouselis, Y. Kwon, Multi-criteria recommender systems. in *Recommender Systems Handbook*, ed. by F. Ricci, L. Rokach, B. Shapira (eds.) (Springer US, 2011), pp. 769–803

P. Brusilovsky, E. Millan, User models for adaptive hypermedia and adaptive educational systems, in *The adaptive web*, vol. 4321, ed. by P. Brusilovsky, et al. (Springer, 2007), pp. 3–53

V. Butoianu, P. Vidal, K. Verbert, E. Duval, J. Broisin, User context and personalized learning: a federation of contextualized attention metadata. J. UCS **16**(16), 2252–2271 (2010)

A. Chervenak, I. Foster, C. Kesselman, C. Salisbury, S. Tuecke, The data grid: towards an architecture for the distributed management and analysis of large scientific data sets. J. Netw. Comput. Appl. **23**(3), 187–200 (2000)

B. Cheung, L. Hui, J. Zhang, S.M. Yiu, SmartTutor: an intelligent tutoring system in web-based adult education. J. Syst. Softw. **68**(1), 11–25 (2003)

M. Deshpande, G. Karypis, Item-based Top-N recommendation algorithms. ACM Trans. Inf. Syst. **22**(1), 143–177 (2004)

H. Drachsler, H.G.K. Hummel, R. Koper, Identifying the goal, user model and conditions of recommender systems for formal and informal learning. J. Digit. Inf. 10(2), 4–24 (2009a)

H. Drachsler, H. Hummel, B. Berg, J. Eshuis, W. Waterink, R. Nadolski, A. Berlanga, N. Boers, R. Koper, Evaluating the effectiveness of personalised recommender systems in learning networks. in *Learning Network Services for Professional Development*, ed. by R. Koper (eds.) (Springer, Berlin Heidelberg, 2009b), pp. 95–113

H. Drachsler, T. Bogers, R. Vuorikari, K. Verbert, E. Duval, N. Manouselis, G. Beham, S. Lindstaedt, H. Stern, M. Friedrich, Issues and considerations regarding sharable data sets for recommender systems in technology enhanced learning. Procedia Comput. Sci. 1(2), 2849–2858 (2010a). doi:10.1016/j.procs.2010.08.010

H. Drachsler, K. Verbert, M.-A. Sicilia, M. Wolpers, N. Manouselis, R. Vuorikari, S. Lindstaedt, F. Fischer, DataTEL—datasets for technology enhanced learning. STELLAR ARV White Paper (2011), http://oa.stellarnet.eu/open-archive/browse?resource=6756_v1. Accessed 12 March 2012

H. Drachsler, L. Rutledge, P. van Rosmalen, H. Hummel, D. Pecceu, T. Arts, E. Hutten, R. Koper, Remashed—an usability study of a recommender system for mash-ups for learning. International Journal of Emerging Technologies in Learning (iJet), Special Issue: ICL2009 MashUps for. Learning 5, 7–11 (2010b)

H. Drachsler, K. Verbert, N. Manouselis, S. Lindstaedt, R. Vuorikari, M. Wolpers, Preface for data-TEL Special Issue on Datasets and Data Supported Learning in Technology-Enhanced Learning. Drachsler H, Verbert K, Manouselis N, Lindstaedt S, Vuorikari R, Wolpers M (eds) International Journal of Technology Enhanced Learning (IJTEL), (to appear)

C. Ghidini, V. Pammer, P. Scheir, L. Serafini, S. Lindstaedt, Aposdle: learn@ work with semantic web technology. Proceedings of ISEMANTICS, pp. 262–269 (2007)

J.L. Herlocker, J.A. Konstan, L.G. Terveen, J.T. Riedl, Evaluating collaborative filtering recommender systems. ACM Trans. Inf. Syst. 22(1), 5–53 (2004)

K. Jack, M. Hristakeva, R. Garcia de Zuniga, M. Granitzer, Mendeley's Open Data for Science and Learning: A Reply to the DataTEL Challenge. International Journal of Technology Enhanced Learning (to appear)

E. Jacquet-Lagreze, Y. Siskos, Preference disaggregation: 20 years of MCDA experience. Eur. J. Oper. Res. 130, 233–245 (2001)

V. Kaptelinin, K. Kuutti, L.J. Bannon, Activity theory: basic concepts and applications, in *Selected papers from the 5th International Conference on Human-Computer Interaction*, ed. by B. Blumenthal, et al. (Springer-Verlag, London, 1995), pp. 89–201

R.L. Keeney, *Value-focused Thinking: A Path to Creative Decisionmaking* (Harvard University Press, Cambridge MA, 1992)

G. King, An introduction to the dataverse network as an infrastructure for data sharing. Sociol. Methods Res. 36(2), 173–199 (2007)

J.A. Konstan, Introduction to recommender systems: algorithms and evaluation. ACM Trans. Inf. Syst. 22(1), 1–4 (2004)

N. Manouselis, H. Drachsler, K. Verbert, O.C. Santos, RecSysTEL preface. Procedia Comput. Sci. 1(2), 2773–2774 (2010a)

N. Manouselis, R. Vuorikari, F. Van Assche, Collaborative recommendation of e-learning resources: an experimental investigation. JCAL 26(4), 227–242 (2010b)

N. Manouselis, (2008) A discussion on multi-criteria recommendation. in *Proceedings of the Workshop on Recommender Systems, 18th European Conference on Artificial Intelligence* (ECAI 2008), Patras, Greece, July, 2008

N. Manouselis, R. Vuorikari, F. Van Assche, Simulated analysis of MAUT collaborative filtering for learning object recommendation. in *Proceedings of the Workshop on Social Information Retrieval in Technology Enhanced Learning* (SIRTEL 2007), Crete, Greece, 2007

N. Manouselis, H. Drachsler, R. Vuorikari, H. Hummel, R. Koper, Recommender Systems in Technology Enhanced Learning, in *Kantor P*, ed. by F. Ricci, L. Rokach, B. Shapira (Recommender Systems Handbook, Springer US, 2011), pp. 387–415

N. Manouselis, K. Kastrantas, S.S. Alonso, J. Caceres, H. Ebner, M. Palmer, Architecture of the organic.Edunet web portal. Int. J. Web Portals 1(1), 71–91 (2009)

G. McCalla, The ecological approach to the design of E-learning environments: purpose-based capture and use of information about learners. Journal of Interactive Media in Education, Special Issue on the Educational Semantic Web, 7, ISSN:1365–893X (2004)

C. Pahl, C. Donnellan, Data mining technology for the evaluation of web-based teaching and learning systems, in *Proceedings of E-Learn 2002*, ed. by M. Driscoll, T. Reeves (AACE, Chesapeake, VA, 2002), pp. 747–752

A. Rath, D. Devaurs, S. Lindstaedt, UICO: an ontology-based user interaction context model for automatic task detection on the computer desktop. in *Proceedings of the 1st Workshop on Context, Information and Ontologies*, p. 10, ACM (2009)

C. Reffay, M.-L. Betbeder, Sharing corpora and tools to improve interaction analysis. in *Proceedings of EC-TEL '09, LNCS*, vol. 5794, ed. by U. Cress, V. Dimitrova, M. Specht (Springer-Verlag, Berlin, Heidelberg, 2009), pp. 196–210

C. Romero, S. Ventura, Educational data mining: a survey from 1995 to 2005. Expert Syst. Appl. **33**(1), 135–146 (2007). Elsevier

C. Romero, S. Ventura, P.G. Espejo, C. Hervs, Data mining algorithms to classify students. in *Proceedings of the 1st International Conference on Educational Data Mining*, ed. by R. de Baker, T. Barnes, J. Beck (eds) pp. 8–17 (2008)

B. Roy, D. Bouyssou, *Aide Multicritere a la Decision: Methodes et Cas* (Economica, Paris, 1993)

B. Roy, *Multicriteria Methodology for Decision Aiding* (Kluwer Academic Publishers, Dordrecht, 1996)

M. Scheffel, K. Niemann, A. Pardo, D. Leony, M. Friedrich, K. Schmidt, M. Wolpers, C.D. Kloos, Usage pattern recognition in student activities. in *Proceedings of EC-TEL'11* (Springer-Verlag, Berlin, Heidelberg, 2011), pp. 341–355

J.C. Stamper, K.R. Koedinger, R. Baker, A. Skogsholm, B. Leber, J. Rankin, S. Demi, PSLC dataShop: a data analysis service for the learning science community. in *Proceedings of Intelligent Tutoring Systems*, vol. 6095, (Springer, 2010), pp. 455–456

T, Tang, G. McCalla, Smart recommendation for an evolving E-learning system. in *Proceedings of the Workshop on Technologies for Electronic Documents for Supporting Learning, International Conference on Artificial Intelligence in Education* (AIED 2003), (2003) pp. 699–710

K. Verbert, H. Drachsler, N. Manouselis, M. Wolpers, R. Vuorikari, E. Duval, Dataset-driven research for improving recommender systems for learning. in *Proceedings of the 1st International Conference on Learning Analytics and Knowledge*, pp. 44–53. ACM, New York, NY, USA. ISBN: 978-1-4503-0944-8, 2011

K. Verbert, N. Manouselis, H. Drachsler, E. Duval, Dataset-driven Research to Support Learning and Knowledge Analytics. Educational Technology and Society, Special Issue on Learning and Knowledge Analytics, (to appear)

R. Vuorikari, Ecology of social search for learning resources. CampusWide Inf. Syst. **26**(4), 272–286 (2009)

L. Vygotsky, *Mind in Society: The Development of Higher Psychological Processes* (Harvard University Press, 1978)

M. Wolpers, M. Memmel, A. Giretti, Metadata in architecture education—first evaluation results of the mace system. Learn. Synerg. Multiple Discipl. **5794**, 112–126 (2009)

M. Zeleny, *Linear Multiobjective Programming* (Spinger, New York, 1974)

Chapter 3
Survey and Analysis of TEL Recommender Systems

Abstract In this chapter, we present a framework for the analysis of existing recommender systems. Then, we present a detailed analysis of relevant TEL recommender systems along the dimensions defined by our framework.

3.1 Framework for Analysis

Several frameworks have been proposed for the analysis of recommender systems. Hanani et al. (2001) conducted a nice review of information filtering issues and systems, and presented a high-level framework for the classification of such systems. The proposed framework included dimensions such as the initiative of operation, the location of operation, and the methods for acquiring knowledge from users. Some dimensions of this framework could be specifically used for the description, analysis and categorisation of recommender systems.

The review and classification of Schafer et al. (2001) focused on the recommender systems of a particular domain, the e-commerce one. Nevertheless, their classification framework (identifying dimensions such as the user inputs, the outputs, the recommendation method, the degree of personalisation, and the delivery mode) can be also applied for systems in other application domains. Another survey that focused particularly on the recommender systems of the e-commerce domain has been the one carried out by Wei et al. (2002). The authors also provided a generic framework for classifying recommender systems, distinguishing dimensions such as the information used for recommendation decisions, the types of recommendation decisions, and the various recommendation techniques.

A survey that focused on the various recommendation techniques, introducing new types of systems apart from the content-based and collaborative ones, has been the one of Burke (2002). His study described in detail the identified recommendation techniques, and compared them in terms of benefits and shortcomings. Furthermore, Montaner et al. (2003) focused specifically on recommender agents, and analysed a number of such systems. Their taxonomy is based on dimensions such as the way the user profile is represented, generated, and adapted to the user preferences. Apart from agent systems, the proposed taxonomy can be used for other, non-agent types of recommender systems as well.

In their study of recommender systems Adomavicius and Tuzhilin (2005) have reviewed the various types of such systems, based on the distinction between content-based, collaborative, and hybrid ones. They provided a very detailed overview of the different techniques used in the context of each system type, in order to support recommendation.

All of the above studies, as well as others that did not focus particularly in categorising recommender systems (e.g. Herlocker et al. 2004; Han et al. 2004), have indicated important dimensions which may be considered for their analysis and classification. Manouselis and Costopoulou (2007a) have collected, elaborated and categorised the dimensions identified in these previous studies into a proposed framework with three main categories of characteristics: *Supported Tasks*, *Approach* and *Operation*. The authors used this framework to analyse and classify 37 multi-criteria recommender systems. We use this framework as a basis for our analysis, extending it slightly as far as the supported tasks are concerned, for the case of TEL recommenders (Fig. 3.1).

First of all, *Supported Tasks* refers to the dimensions that distinguish recommender systems according to the user tasks that they are meant to support (Herlocker et al. 2004). The main supported tasks for TEL recommender systems have been discussed in Chap. 2, and from them we can highlight the following:

- *Find Novel Resources*: recommendations of particularly new or novel items, e.g. receiving very new and/or controversial resources on covered topics.
- *Find Peers*: recommendation of other people with relevant interests, e.g. being suggested profiles of users with similar interests or being suggested students in the same class or a peer student in a learning network.
- *Find Good Pathways*: recommendation of alternative learning paths through learning resources, e.g. receiving a list of alternative learning paths over the same resources to achieve a learning goal depending.
- *Predict Student Performance*: data mining techniques are also used to create recommendations but with the emerging research around learning analytics and educational data mining these techniques are used to predict learning performance of learners as well as the teaching qualities of teachers.

The *Approach* category includes three different perspectives, in accordance to the system components that related research in personalised/adaptive systems distinguishes (that is, systems that adapt some part of their operation according to the needs or preferences of each particular user) (Brusilovsky 1996). These are:

1. *User Model.* The user model (or user profile) refers to the ways that user characteristics are represented, stored and updated in a recommender system. The following dimensions can be identified:

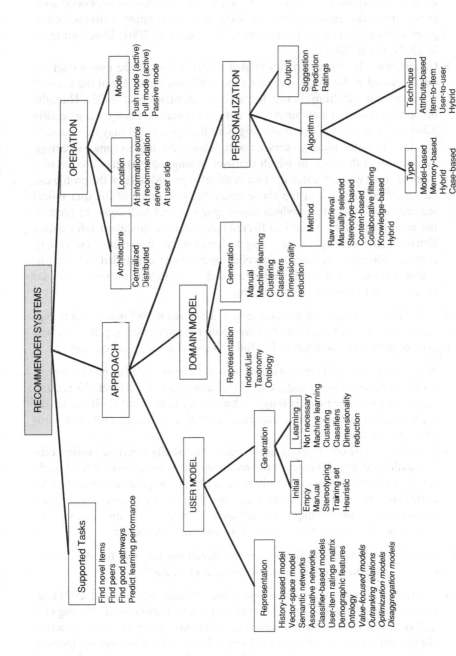

Fig. 3.1 Framework for the analysis (adapted from Manouselis and Costopoulou 2007a)

- *Representation.* The user model can be performed using several methods that include: history-based models, vector space models, semantic networks, associative networks, classifier-based models, user-items rating matrixes, demographic features, as well as ontologies (Schafer et al. 2001; Montaner et al. 2003; Wei et al. 2002).

- *Generation.* The characteristics related to generation of the user model are distinguished in the ways of creating the initial user model, and the ways of learning the model from some collected data (Montaner et al. 2003). Thus, the initial user model in a recommender system (a) may be empty and gradually filled while the user starts interacting with the system, (b) may be manually provided from the user, (c) may be completed according to some stereotype that describes the class in which the user belongs, or (d) may consist of a training set of examples that the user is asked to provide so that the profile can be generated. In some of the above cases, the generation of the user model requires a learning phase, which may engage several techniques to produce the user model from initially collected data, such as structured Information Retrieval (IR) techniques, clustering techniques, latent semantic analysis, or some classification technique. This phase may be also concluded by the application of some dimensionality reduction technique, to limit the size of the user model and thus simplify its processing.

2. *Domain Model.* Similarly to the user model, a domain model is required to represent the properties of the items that are being recommended, e.g. the products in an e-commerce recommender. The following dimensions can be identified:

   - *Representation.* The items in the domain may be represented using (a) a simple index or catalog of items that are all at the same hierarchical level, (b) a taxonomy of items where items belong to a hierarchy of classes of similar items, or (c) an ontology where more complex relationships are defined between items or classes of items.

   - *Generation.* The descriptions of the items are usually generated using techniques that are beyond the scope of a recommender system. Sometimes though, a recommender system may apply some technique to generate/formulate the appropriate representation from some raw data or other representation that describes the items. Examples of such techniques are association rule mining, clustering, classification, as well as, dimensionality reduction.

3. *Personalisation.* It refers to dimensions that depict the way that the system provides its recommendations, in terms of (Schafer et al. 2001):

   - *Method.* The recommendation methods may include (Schafer et al. 2001): (a) raw retrieval of items where no particular personalisation method is engaged and recommended items are presented as results of typical search queries; (b) manual selection of recommendations, for example when some experts or opinion-leaders recommend a list of items to all users, e.g. Amazon's recommendations such as this author recommends the following books; (c) content-based recommendation methods which characterise the contents of the item and the information needs of potential item users, and then use these representations to match items to users; (d) collaborative filtering recommendation methods that recommend items to a user according to what people with similar tastes and preferences liked in the past; as well as, (e) hybrid approaches that combine some of the above methods.

- *Type.* May include model-based algorithms, memory-based or heuristic-based algorithms, and hybrid algorithms (Adomavicius and Tuzhilin 2005).
- *Technique.* Algorithms may adopt attribute-based techniques, item-to-item correlation techniques, or user-to-user techniques (Schafer et al. 2001).
- *Output.* The most common recommendation outputs are suggestions (e.g. 'try this item'), original ratings or reviews that other people provided about a particular item, or predictions of the ratings that user would give to recommended items (Schafer et al. 2001).

The *Operation* category also includes three different perspectives that include dimensions related to the deployment of recommender systems:

1. *Architecture.* It refers to the architecture of the recommender system, which is usually distinguished as (Miller et al. 2004; Han et al. 2004):

   - *Centralised.* When the recommender system is at one particular location.
   - *Distributed.* When the system components are distributed to more locations, e.g. in the case of peer-to-peer architectures.

2. *Location.* It refers to the location where recommendation is produced and delivered. It can be classified according to the following locations (Hanani et al. 2001):

   - *At information source.* The case when the information source or provider provides a recommender system to its users, e.g. an e-market provides a product recommendation service. The user profile is stored at the information source side.
   - *At recommendation server.* Recommendations are provided from a third-party entity, referring to various external information sources, e.g. when restaurants are recommended to interested users by an independent recommender system. The user profile is stored at the recommendation server.
   - *At user side.* The user profile is stored at the user's side, and the recommendations are locally produced, e.g. in the case of an e-mail filtering system.

3. *Mode.* It concerns the identification of who initiates the recommendation process, distinguished among (Herlocker et al. 2004; Schafer et al. 2001):

   - *Push mode (active).* Recommendations are 'pushed' to the user even when the user is not interacting with the system, e.g. via e-mail.
   - *Pull mode (active).* Recommendations are produced, but are presented to the user only when he allows or requests it.
   - *Passive mode.* Recommendations are produced as part of the regular system operation, e.g. as product recommendations when the user visits an e-market.

In the next section, we use this framework to analyse a sample of 42 TEL recommenders that we identified from the past 10 years of research.

3.2 Survey Results

3.2.1 General Overview of Sample

In the TEL domain a number of recommender systems have been introduced in order to propose learning resources to users. Such systems could potentially play an important educational role, considering the variety of learning resources that are published online and the benefits of collaboration between tutors and learners (Recker and Wiley 2001; Kumar et al. 2005).

The following section reviews a sample of TEL recommender systems that have been proposed in the literature over a period of ten years, and provides an assessment of their status of development and evaluation. In Table 3.1 an overview of this sample of 42 systems is provided, together with an **[RSx]** number that we indicatively use to identify them uniquely and easily in the remainder of this chapter.

One of the first attempts to develop a collaborative filtering system for learning resources has been the Altered Vista system **[RS1]** (Recker and Walker 2003; Recker et al. 2003; Walker et al. 2004). The aim of this study was to explore how to collect user-provided evaluations of learning resources, and then to propagate them in the form of word-of-mouth recommendations about the qualities of the resources. The team working on Altered Vista explored several relevant issues, such as the design of its interface and the development of non-authoritative metadata to store user-provided evaluations (Recker and Wiley 2001), the design of the system and the review scheme it uses (Recker and Walker 2003), as well as results from pilot and empirical studies from using the system to recommend to the members of a community both interesting resources and people with similar tastes and beliefs (Recker et al. 2003; Walker et al. 2004).

Another system that has been proposed for the recommendation of learning resources is the RACOFI **[RS2]** (Rule-Applying Collaborative Filtering) Composer system (Anderson et al. 2003; Lemire 2005; Lemire et al. 2005). RACOFI combines two recommendation approaches by integrating a collaborative filtering engine, that works with ratings that users provide for learning resources, with an inference rule engine that is mining association rules between the learning resources and using them for recommendation. RACOFI studies have not yet assessed the pedagogical value of the recommender, nor do they report some evaluation of the system by users. The RACOFI technology is supporting the commercial site inDiscover (http://www.indiscover.net) for music tracks recommendation. In addition, other researchers have reported adopting RACOFI's approach in their own systems as well (Fiaidhi 2004).

The QSIA **[RS3]** (Questions Sharing and Interactive Assignments) for learning resources sharing, assessing and recommendation has been developed by Rafaeli

Table 3.1 Implemented TEL systems reported in literature

System	Status	Evaluator focus	Evaluation roles
[RS1] Altered Vista (Recker et al. 2000; Recker and Wiley 2001; Recker and Walker 2003; Recker et al. 2003; Walker et al. 2004)	Full system	Interface, algorithm, system usage	Human users
[RS2] RACOFI (Anderson et al. 2003; Lemire 2005)	Prototype	Algorithm	System designers
[RS3] QSIA (Rafaeli et al. 2004, 2005)	Full system	–	–
[RS4] CYCLADES (Avancini and Straccia 2005)	Full system	Algorithm	System designers
[RS5] CoFind (Dron et al. 2000a,b)	Prototype	System usage	Human users
[RS6] Learning object sequencing (Shen and Shen 2004)	Prototype	System usage	Human users
[RS7] Evolving e-learning system (Tang and McCalla 2003, 2004a,b,c, 2005)	Full system	Algorithm, System usage	Simulated users, Human users
[RS8] ISIS—Hybrid Personalised Recommender System (Drachsler et al. 2009c)	Prototype	Algorithm, system usage	Human users
[RS9] Multi-Attribute Recommendation Service (Manouselis et al. 2007, 2010)	Prototype	Algorithm	System designers
[RS10] Learning Object Recommendation Model (Tsai et al. 2006)	Design	–	–
[RS11] RecoSearch (Fiaidhi 2004)	Design	–	–
[RS12] Simulation environment (Nadolski et al. 2009)	Full system	Algorithm	Simulated users
[RS13] ReMashed (Drachsler et al. 2009a,b)	Full system	Interface, algorithm, system usage	Human users
[RS14] CourseRank (Koutrika et al. 2008, 2009)	Full system	Interface, algorithm, system usage	Human users
[RS15] CBR Recommender Interface (Gomez-Albarran and Jimenez-Diaz 2009)	Prototype	–	–
[RS16] APOSDLE People Recommender Service (Aehnelt et al. 2008; Beham et al. 2010)	Full system	Interface, algorithm, system usage	Human users
[RS17] A2M Recommending System (Santos 2008)	Prototype	–	–
[RS18] Moodle Recommender System (Janssen et al. 2005)	Prototype	Interface, algorithm, system usage	Human users
[RS19] LRLS (Huang et al. 2009)	Prototype	Interface, algorithm, system usage	Human users
[RS20] CLICK (Okoye et al. 2012)	Prototype	Interface, algorithm, system usage	System designers

(Continued)

Table 3.1 (continued)

System	Status	Evaluator focus	Evaluation roles
[RS21] Ontology network for Semantic Educational Recommender Systems (Diaz et al. 2012)	Concept	Algorithm	–
[RS22] Recommender System for Learning Objects (Casali et al. 2012)	Prototype	Algorithm, system usage	–
[RS23] Meta-Mender (Zaldivar et al. 2012; Zaldivar and Burgos 2010)	Prototype	Interface algorithm	–
[RS24] Recommender System for Meta-Cognitive Functioning (Zhou and Xu 2012)	Concept	Algorithm	–
[RS25] PLE Recommender System (Moedritscher 2010)	Concept	Algorithm	–
[RS26] Lecture slides Recommender System (Wang and Sumiya 2010)	Prototype	Algorithm, system usage	–
[RS27] Recommender System based on educational data mining (Thai-Nghe et al. 2010)	Concept	Algorithm, system usage	–
[RS28] Exercise Recommender System (Michlik and Bielikova 2010)	Full system	Interface, algorithm, system usage	Human users
[RS29] Work-based learning recommendations (Schoefegger et al. 2010)	Concept	Algorithm, system usage	–
[RS30] Recommender System based on CAM (Broisin et al. 2010)	Prototype	Interface, algorithm, system usage	–
[RS31] Recommender System for learning objects (Sicilia et al. 2010)	Concept	Algorithm, system usage	–
[RS32] OpenCourseWare Recommender (Shelton et al. 2010)	Full system	Interface, algorithm, system usage	–
[RS33] Competence based Recommender Systems (Marino and Paquette 2010)	Prototype	Interface, algorithm, system usage	Human users
[RS34] Recommender System for Social Navigation in Digital Libraries (Brusilovsky et al. 2010)	Full system	Interface, algorithm, system usage	–
[RS35] Factorization Techniques for Predicting Student Performance (Thai-Nghe et al. 2012)	Concept	Algorithm, system usage	–
[RS36] idSpace Recommender System (Sielis et al. 2012)	Prototype	Interface, algorithm, system usage	Human users
[RS37] Metis (Underwood 2012)	Prototype	Algorithm	–
[RS38] RPL recommender (Khribi et al. 2009)	Prototype	System usage	System designers, Human users

(Continued)

Table 3.1 (continued)

System	Status	Evaluator focus	Evaluation roles
[RS39] Comparison of collaborative filtering algorithms on different educational data sets (Verbert et al. 2011)	Concept	Algorithm, system usage	–
[RS40] Bibliography Meta-search engine (Bodea et al. 2012)	Full system	Interface, algorithm, system usage	Human users
[RS41] CourseAgent (Farzan and Brusilovsky 2010)	Full system	System usage	Human users
[RS42] 3A recommender (El Helou et al. 2010)	Prototype	Algorithm	System designers

et al. (2004, 2005). This system is used in the context of online communities, in order to harness the social perspective in learning and to promote collaboration, online recommendation, and further formation of learner communities. Instead of developing a typical automated recommender system, Rafaeli et al. chose to base QSIA on a mostly user-controlled recommendation process. That is, the user can decide whether to assume control on who advises (friends) or to use a collaborative filtering service. The system has been implemented and used in the context of several learning situations, such as knowledge sharing among faculty and teaching assistants, high school teachers and among students, but no evaluation results have been reported so far (Rafaeli et al. 2004, 2005).

In this strand of systems for collaborative filtering of learning resources, the CYCLADES system **[RS4]** (Avancini and Straccia 2005) has proposed an environment where users search, access, and evaluate (rate) digital resources available in repositories found through the Open Archives Initiative OAI (Lagoze and Van de Sompel (2001)). Informally, OAI is an agreement between several digital archives providers in order to offer some minimum level of interoperability between them. Thus, such a system can offer recommendations over resources that are stored in different archives and accessed through an open scheme. The recommendations offered by CYCLADES have been evaluated through a pilot study with about 60 users, which focused on testing the performance (predictive accuracy) of several collaborative filtering algorithms.

A related system is the CoFind prototype **[RS5]** (Dron et al. 2000a,b). It also used digital resources that are freely available on the Web but it followed a new approach by applying for the first time folksonomies (tags) for recommendations. The CoFind developers stated that predictions according to preferences were inadequate in a learning context and therefore more user driven bottom-up categories like folksonomies are important.

A typical, neighborhood-based set of collaborative filtering algorithms have been tried in order to support learning object recommendation by Manouselis et al. (2007, 2010) **[RS9]**. The innovative aspect of this study is that the engaged algorithms have been multi-attribute ones, allowing the recommendation service to consider multi-dimensional ratings that users provide on learning resources. An interesting outcome from this study in comparison to initial experiments using the same algorithms (e.g. Manouselis and Costopoulou 2007b), is that it seems that the performance of the same algorithms is changing, depending on the context where testing takes place. For instance, the results from the comparative study of the same algorithms in an e-commerce (Manouselis and Costopoulou 2007b) and a TEL setting (Manouselis et al. 2007) has led to the selection of different algorithms from the same set of candidate ones. This can be an indicator that the performance of recommendation algorithms that have been proved to be performing well in one context (e.g. movie recommendation) should not be expected to do the same in another context (e.g. TEL), an area which requires further experimentation.

A similar approach is followed by the proposed Learning Object Recommendation Model (LORM) **[RS10]** that also follows a hybrid recommendation algorithmic approach and that describes resources upon multiple attributes, but has not yet reported to be implemented in an actual system (Tsai et al. 2006). This research direction was recently followed up by Sicilia et al. (2010) **[RS31]** with a data set from the learning object repository MERLOT and Verbert et al. (2011) **[RS39]** with a collection of different TEL data sets (see also Chap. 2) and the Mahout recommender framework.[1] Both studies demonstrated the effects of different collaborative filtering techniques on TEL data sets, while Sicilia et al. (2010) **[RS31]** also investigated multi-criteria ratings like Manouselis et al. (2007, 2010) in **[RS9]** to recommend learning resources. All papers applied collaborative filtering techniques on the TEL data sets but did not design a specific solution for the TEL context.

Casali et al. (2012) **[RS22]** tried to take the needs and preferences of learners into account. They describe a recommender system that suggests suitable learning objects from distribute learning repositories by applying personalised search agents. The developed agents are following an hybrid recommendation approach by combining content- and knowledge-based techniques.

A different approach to recommend learning resources based on learner needs has been followed by Shen and Shen (2004) **[RS6]**. They have developed a recommender system for learning objects that is based on sequencing rules that help users to be guided through the concepts of an ontology of topics. The rules are fired when gaps in the competences of the learners are identified and search for appropriate resources to train these gaps. A pilot study with the students of a Network Education college has taken place, providing feedback regarding the users' opinion about the system. Such top-down ontology and other semantic driven recommender approaches are applied frequently for TEL recommender systems especially. when the systems take into account specific domain and user information like knowledge-levels. Another reason to apply ontology and semantic techniques is the lack of large educational data sets that are needed to techniques like collaborative filtering in an efficient and accurate way. In this context, rule- and ontology based recommender systems seem to be an effective solution because they can offer specific recommendations even with very little user information available. A disadvantage of ontology- and rule-based

---

[1] http://mahout.apache.org

recommender systems is their high maintain effort, reengineer, and adaptation to user and domain preferences. Most of the time the development of the domain ontology and the domain concept map is done manually by experts and requires high efforts in terms of expertise, time and money. Thus, such systems are difficult to replicate for other domains and hence the benefits of the system are not easily transferred. In the following paragraph we summarise shortly the systems that belong to this cluster. At the end of the paragraph we will present some innovative approaches that tend to overcome the manual editing by domain experts and are therefore promising of the TEL domain.

The METIS system **[RS37]** (Underwood 2012) recommends learning activities in the domain of math based on prior knowledge, skills, and abilities (KSA) of the learners. It uses a structured map of mathematical concepts and maps this with the KSA factor of the learners. A similar approach was taken by Marino and Paquette (2010) **[RS33]**. The authors presented a multi-agent system that gives advice on tasks and resources based on competence driven user models and on ontology-based multi-actor learning flows. Michlik and Bielikova (2010) **[RS28]** propose a method for personalised recommendation of assignments (tasks or exercises) in an adaptive educational system. Their main goal is to help students to achieve better performance in tests. To achieve this objective, they enhanced existing adaptive navigation approaches by considering the limited time for learning. The proposed method uses utility-based recommending and concept-based knowledge modelling.

A related technology is applied in the Meta-Mender recommendation system **[RS23]** (Zaldivar and Burgos 2010; Zaldivar et al. 2012) that applies meta-rules consisting of a set of rules to personalise the information to the learner. These rules are in most cases written by domain experts and can be applied without any user tracking data available. Related approaches like the system presented by Diaz et al. (2012) **[RS21]** apply a network of ontologies that conceptualise different domains and their characteristics to provide semantic recommendations. Sielis et al. (2012) **[RS36]** apply ontologies to support creativity with a recommender system that suggests creativity techniques to the users. The recommended pattern is ontology-driven and based on problem parameters the user is trying to solve (e.g. type of the problem, problem definition, problem complexity, if the problem is divisible, objectives, if expert knowledge is required, etc.). These recommendations are provided to users during the ideation process within the idSpace platform. They applied topic map technology for storing, managing, and delivering content used as recommendations. Bodea et al. (2012) **[RS40]** present one of the more innovative and flexible ontology-driven recommender systems. They combined an e-assessment task with a meta-search engine. Based on the outcomes of the e-assessment the learners get web pages recommended that match to the identified knowledge gaps form the learners. The clustering process uses an educational ontology and WordNet lexical database to create its categories that are forwarded to a meta-search engine. Similarly, the CLICK recommender system (Okoye et al. 2012) **[RS20]** also suggests resources to learners based on knowledge gaps identified by comparing automatically generated domain and learner models. The system provides recommendations from distributed learning repositories based on concept knowledge of the users derived from automated evaluation from essay writing. It is specialised for recommendations of scientific contents.

Another advanced ontology driven recommender system with vector-based similarity measures is presented by Broisin et al. (2010) **[RS30]**. They present a solution for recommending documents to students according to their current activity that is tracked in terms of semantic annotations associated to the accessed resources. Their approach is based on an existing tracking system that captures the current activity of the user in a profile that presents the current interests in an ontology. The recommender service builds upon this user profile and Contextualized Attention Metadata (CAM) that contains the annotation of documents accessed by all users. The user profile is updated as soon as an activity is completed; thus, recommendations provided by the service are up-to-date in real time. The original aspect of this recommendation approach consists in combining a user activity tracking system with the exploitation of the semantic annotations associated with resources.

A similar approach was followed by Wang and Sumiya (2010) **[RS26]**. They developed a content retrieval method involving the semantic ranking of lecture slides based on the relations between slides search needs of the users. This method uses keywords instead of activities and creates conceptual relationship between the extracted keywords from the slides text and the search query keywords of the users. Their semantic ranking method provides suitable slides for their information needs.

Schoefegger et al. (2010) **[RS29]** present a fresh approach to recommend resources at the workplace. They apply a context driven recommender system to effectively support knowledge workers to meet their individual information needs. They focus on adapting the current context of a knowledge worker in a representative user model that contains information like interest and knowledge-levels. The authors present an approach to model the users' context based on the emerging topics rather than fixed domain topics by extracting tagging information from the user's past activities within the system.

An ontology independent approach that also applies meta-rules but derived from a Markov chain model was presented by Huang et al. (2009) **[RS19]**. It uses a Markov chains to calculate transition probabilities of possible learning objects in a sequenced course of study. The model is supported by an entropy-based approach for discovering one or more recommended learning paths. A pilot implementation has been deployed and tested in a Taiwanese university, involving about 150 users.

Tang and McCalla proposed an evolving e-learning system, open into new learning resources that may be found online, which includes a hybrid recommendation service **[RS7]** (Tang and McCalla 2003, 2004a,b,c, 2005). Their system is mainly used for storing and sharing research papers and glossary terms among university students and industry practitioners. Resources are described (tagged) according to their content and technical aspects, but learners also provide feedback about them in the form of ratings. Recommendation takes place both by engaging a Clustering Module (using data clustering techniques to group learners with similar interests) and a Collaborative Filtering Module (using classic collaborative filtering techniques to identify learners with similar interests in each cluster). The authors studied several techniques to enhance the performance of their system, such as the usage of artificial (simulated) learners (Tang and McCalla 2004c). They have also performed an evaluation study of the system with real learners (Tang and McCalla 2005). The work of Tang and McCalla has been evaluated in learning settings and is included in our analysis. Many other recommenders have been developed that support recommendation of scientific papers. Examples include work of Sie et al. (to appear). The authors followed a different approach and suggested suitable co-authors for scientific article writing based on weak and strong ties in a bibliographic network. The network information (betweenness centrality) and author (keyword) similarity are used to compute the utility of peers in the network of co-authors. While these systems have many commonalities with TEL recommenders, we focus in this chapter specifically on recommenders that have been used in learning settings.

A rather straightforward approach that does not take into account preferences or profile information of the learners is adopted by Janssen et al. (2005) **[RS18]**. However, they conducted a large experiment with a control group and an experimental group. They found positive effects on the effectiveness (completion rates of learning objects) though not on efficiency (time taken to complete the learning resources) for the experimental group as compared to the control group.

Nadolski et al. (2009) **[RS12]** created a simulation environment for different combination of recommendation algorithms in hybrid recommender systems in order to compare them against each other regarding their impact on learners in informal learning networks. They compared various cost intensive ontology based recommendation strategies with light-weight collaborative filtering strategies. Therefore, they created treatment groups for the simulation through combining the recommendation techniques in various ways. Nadolski et al. (2009) tested which combination of recommendation techniques in recommendation strategies had a higher effect on the learning outcomes of the learners in a learning network. They concluded that the light-weight collaborative filtering recommendation strategies are not as accurate as the ontology-based strategies but worth-while for informal learning networks when considering the environmental conditions like the lack of maintenance in learning networks. This study confirmed that providing recommendations leads towards more effective, more satisfied, and faster goal achievement than no recommendation. Furthermore, their study reveals that a light-weight collaborative filtering recommendation technique including a rating mechanism is a good alternative to maintain intensive top-down ontology recommendation techniques.

Moreover, the ISIS system **[RS8]** that adopts a hybrid approach for recommending learning resources is the one recently proposed by Hummel et al. (2007). The authors build upon a previous simulation study by Koper (2005) in order to propose a system that combines social-based (using data from other learners) with information-based (using metadata from learner profiles and learning activities) in a hybrid recommender system. They also designed an experiment with real learners. Drachsler et al. (2009c) reported experimental results with ISIS. They found a positive significant effect on efficiency (time taken to complete the learning objects) of the learners after a runtime of four months. It is a very good example of a system that is following the latest trends in learning specifications for representing learner profiles and learning activities.

Based on the promising findings of the simulations, the same group developed the ReMashed recommender system (Drachsler et al. 2009a,b) **[RS13]** that focuses on learners in informal learning networks. They created a mash-up environment that combines sources of users from different Web2.0 services like Flickr, Delicious.com or Sildeshare.com. Again, they applied a hybrid recommender system that takes advantage of the tag and rating data of the combined Web2.0 sources. The tags that are already given to the Web2.0 sources are used for the cold-start of the recommender system (Marinho et al. 2010). The users of ReMashed are able to rate the emerging data of all users in the system. The ratings are used for classic collaborative filtering recommendations based on the Duine prediction engine (Van Setten 2005). The research on recommender systems for mash-up environments is closely related to research on Personal Learning Environments (PLEs) (Friedrich et al. 2011). PLEs can also result in an information overflow if too many sources are connected to it or too many widgets can be combined for a certain task. Moedritscher (2010) **[RS25]** and El Helou et al. (2010) **[RS42]** recently presented a recommendation strategy and a small-scale experiment to provide recommender system for these kinds of learning environments. The 3A recommender **[RS42]** (El Helou et al. 2010) targets context-aware recommendation in personal learning environments. Context is measured and represented by different types of relations, including social relations and relations between resources. The 3A recommendation algorithm adapts a version of Google's PageRank algorithm to the particular modelling framework that considers relation context. Evaluation results indicate that the incorporation of relations outperforms standard collaborative filtering in terms of recall.

Another hybrid recommendation approach has been adopted in the CourseRank system **[RS14]** (Koutrika et al. 2008) that is used as an alternative curriculum planner and course guide for Stanford University students. In this system, the recommendation process is viewed under the prism of querying a relational database with course and student information (Koutrika et al. 2008). To this end, a number of operators have been defined in order to allow the system to provide flexible recommendations to its users. The system has been first deployed in September 2007, attracting lots of interest from the students: it has been reported that more than 70 % of the Stanford students are using the system (Koutrika et al. 2009).

CourseAgent **[RS41]** (Farzan and Brusilovsky 2010) is another example of a recommender system that relies on a hybrid approach to recommend courses. The system has been used at the University of Pittsburgh and has been evaluated based on a long-term evaluation experiment with students. A hybrid approach is also adopted by the prototype system that has been implemented in the course repository of the Virtual University of Tunis (RPL platform **[RS38]**[2]). This prototype includes a recommendation engine that combines a collaborative filtering algorithm with a content-based filtering algorithm, using data that has been logged and mined from user actions. The usage logs of the RPL platform are used for this purpose, and a preliminary evaluation experiment has already taken place (Khribi et al. 2009).

---

[2] http://cours.uvt.rnu.tn/rpl/

There have been some articles about systems or algorithms that could be used to support recommendation of learning resources and peer recommendations that apply hybrid recommendation approaches. These include a variety of work-in-progress systems, such as a case-based reasoning recommender of Gomez-Albarran and Jimenez-Diaz (2009) **[RS15]**, the contextual recommendations that the knowledge-sharing environment of the APOSDLE EU-project **[RS16]** offers to the employees of large organisations (Aehnelt et al. 2008; Beham et al. 2010), and the A2M prototype **[RS7]** (Santos 2008). Lastly, recommendation of multimedia learning resource onto mobile devices such as cell phones and PDAs have been explored in Klamma et al. (2006).

One of the most known and frequently used recommender systems is the Open-CourseWare recommender system reported in Shelton et al. (2010) **[RS32]**. The OpenCourseWare recommender supports teachers and learners to find relevant learning objects from a growing number of different digital libraries and open education repositories. They present the design and evaluation of Folksemantic, a system that integrates OpenCourseWare search, Open Educational Resources and vector-based similarity based on the Lucene "more like this" function. With this approach, they created personalised recommendation functionality of different repositories in a single open source project. An alternative approach for navigation support in the increasing amount of digital libraries and repositories was presented by Brusilovsky et al. (2010) **[RS34]**. The authors address the concrete issue, that with the growth of the volume and the diversity of the library, it becomes increasingly difficult for the users to find resources, which are relevant to their personal context (age, educational needs, and personal interests). Social navigation techniques could provide valuable help to guide users to the most useful information. Their social navigation approach builds upon traces of past user behavior and using the assembled collective wisdom to guide future users. Next to recommending 'Find Novel Items' the system offers also opportunities to 'Find Pathways' (learning paths) based on the Walden path concept. Most of the recommender systems described above had the TEL recommendation task to either 'Find Novel Items', 'Find Peers', or 'Find Pathways' to their target user. Thai-Nghe et al. (2012) **[RS27]** introduce an additional recommendation task to the field: 'Predict Student Performance'. This data mining driven approach shows the overlap between the TEL recommender system research field, the newly emerging Learning Analytics field (Drachsler and Greller 2012), and the already longer existing educational data mining field (Stamper 2011). Going beyond student performance, Thai-Nghe et al. (2012) try to recommend most suitable items in a flexible and personalised manner. They apply factorisation techniques to generate accurate ratings and performance predictions. These techniques are relatively new to the field and are promising as they can effectively address pedagogical requirements as describe in Chap. 1, because they can take temporal effects into account and therefore accurately model and adjust to the increasing knowledge of learners. The authors prove in data-driven experiments that the applied factorisation approach improved the prediction results. This can be very useful in cases where recommended items need to be one level above the current knowledge-level of a learner, according to Vygotsky's *zone of proximal development* (Vygotsky 1978). In a related research study, Thai-Nghe et al. (2010) **[RS35]** propose another approach which uses educational data min-

Table 3.2 Classification of TEL recommenders, according to the Supported Tasks

	Supported tasks
Find Novel Items	[RS1], [RS2], [RS3], [RS4], [RS5], [RS8], [RS9], [RS10], [RS11], [RS13], [RS14], [RS16], [RS20], [RS21], [RS22], [RS23], [RS24], [RS25], [RS26], [RS28], [RS29], [RS30], [RS31], [RS32], [RS33], [RS34], [RS36], [RS38], [RS39], [RS40], [RS41], [RS42]
Find peers	[RS1], [RS4], [RS16], [RS29], [RS36], [RS42]
Find pathways	[RS6], [RS18], [RS19], [RS34], [RS37]
Predict student performance	[RS27], [RS35]
Most suitable learning strategies	[RS24]

ing techniques for recommender systems to predict the performance of students. To validate this approach, they present a comparison study with traditional regression methods such as logistic/linear regression by using educational data for intelligent tutoring systems.

Zhou and Xu (2012) **[RS24]** introduce another new recommendation task to TEL recommender systems, they do not focus on 'Find Novel Items' they focus on recommending 'Most suitable learning strategies' for individual learners. Those learning strategies also known as meta-cognitive functions are important for effective learning processes. A TEL recommender could guide the learner and intelligently recommend learning activities or strategies to facilitate monitoring and control of their own learning. The authors identify the five challenges that need to be overcome and suggest to adopt data mining algorithms like content-based and sequence-based recommendation techniques to meet the identified challenges.

3.2.2 Analysis According to Framework

From the analysis of the supported tasks illustrated in Table 3.2, we can identify that the vast majority of the analysed TEL recommender systems aim to support the task of 'Finding Novel Items' to support learning activities. There have been some applications that aim to support other types of user tasks, but they are still limited. Six of the surveyed systems support 'Find Peers' in addition to recommendation of resources. 'Finding Pathways' through resources and recommending a sequence adapted to the current needs of the learner is supported by six more systems. A few systems rely on recommendation task to 'Predict Student Performance'. The 'Most Suitable Learning Strategies' recommendation task has been introduced by Zhou and Xu (2012) and implemented in **[RS24]**.

From the analysis of the user models that is illustrated in Table 3.3, the following aspects can be identified:

• Most of the methods of the identified TEL recommender systems use classic 'Vector-space models' with multiple attributes to represent the desired features or the user preferences. In addition, many systems rely on 'User-item ratings

Table 3.3 Classification of TEL recommenders, according to the User Model of the Approach category

Approach: User Model			
Representation	Method	Vector-space models	[RS3], [RS4], [RS5], [RS6], [RS10], [RS11], [RS14], [RS20], [RS26], [RS32], [RS35], [RS38], [RS40], [RS41]
		User-item ratings models	[RS1], [RS2], [RS8], [RS9], [RS13], [RS34], [RS41]
		Associative networks	[RS16]
		History-based	[RS8], [RS19], [RS42]
		Ontology	[RS8], [RS21], [RS22], [RS23], [RS24], [RS26], [RS28], [RS30], [RS33], [RS36], [RS37]
	Type	Measurable	[RS1], [RS3], [RS4], [RS5], [RS6], [RS9], [RS10], [RS11], [RS14], [RS16], [RS38]
		Ordinal/features	[RS5]
		Probabilistic	[RS4]
Generation	Initial	Empty	[RS1], [RS2], [RS4], [RS5], [RS14], [RS17]
		Manual	[RS9], [RS27], [RS31], [RS34], [RS39], [RS41], [RS42]
	Learning	Clustering	[RS38]
		Classifiers	[RS4], [RS16], [RS25], [RS29]

models' that capture explicit ratings of users on items. Increasingly, ontology-based representations are used that capture various attributes of users and relationships between those attributes.

- The initial user preferences engaged by the examined systems are usually acquired in a 'Manual' way from the users. In many cases, the user model is initially 'Empty', and then slowly created throughout the users' interactions with the system. Few TEL recommendation systems engage some way (e.g. 'Clustering' or 'Classification') for building the initial model from existing raw data.

Analysing the collected systems on the domain model characteristics (Table 3.4), the following aspects can be identified:

- The majority of the methods of the TEL recommender systems is the simple 'Index/List' for the items being recommended. Only a few systems engage a 'Taxonomy' or a 'Vector-space' of items method. Interestingly, many of the recently introduced recommender systems for learning rely on ontology representations of domain models.
- As it has been probably expected, the domain model is usually created in a 'Manual' way, since only a few of the recommender systems use some technique to

Table 3.4 Classification of TEL recommenders, according to the Domain Model

Approach: Domain Model		
Representation	Index/list	**[RS1]**, **[RS3]**, **[RS4]**, **[RS11]**, **[RS9]**, **[RS14]**, **[RS19]**, **[RS32]**, **[RS38]**, **[RS41]**
	Taxonomy	**[RS5]**, **[RS42]**
	Vector-space model	**[RS26]**, **[RS35]**
	Ontology	**[RS6]**, **[RS8]**, **[RS21]**, **[RS22]**, **[RS23]**, **[RS24]**, **[RS26]**, **[RS28]**, **[RS30]**, **[RS33]**, **[RS36]**, **[RS37]**, **[RS40]**
Generation	Manual	**[RS3]**, **[RS4]**, **[RS5]**, **[RS6]**, **[RS9]**, **[RS11]**, **[RS13]**, **[RS14]**, **[RS27]**, **[RS31]**, **[RS34]**, **[RS39]**
	Classifiers	**[RS16]**, **[RS20]**, **[RS25]**, **[RS38]**
	Clustering	**[RS16]**, **[RS29]**

automatically extract item information from existing sources. A few systems automate metadata generation with classification or clustering methods.

Similarly, Table 3.5 presents the analysis of the TEL recommender systems based on the 'Personalisation' aspect:

- *Method.* In terms of methods used for the personalisation of recommendations, 'Content-based' and 'Collaborative filtering' techniques prevail. The content-based systems have been identified to be more than the collaborative filtering ones, and only a few 'Hybrid' approaches currently exist. Many recent systems rely on ontology-based approaches.
- *Algorithm.* The algorithms used in TEL recommenders are mainly 'Model-based', although many 'Memory-based' ones exist as well. There are also some 'Hybrid' algorithmic approaches. As far as the engaged techniques, most algorithms seem to be employing 'User-to-user' ones. Few 'item-to-item' correlation approaches and 'Attribute-based' ones have been proposed in TEL recommender systems.
- *Output.* The produced output is most of the times in the form of suggested items ('Suggestion'), but there are also systems that try to predict the evaluation that a user would give to the suggested items ('Prediction').

Concerning the 'Operation' category of dimensions, Table 3.6 indicates that:

- *Architecture.* The majority of TEL recommender systems have a 'Centralised' architecture. Although some systems like CYCLADES **[RS4]** (Avancini and Straccia 2005) rely on distributed architectures that provide access to a wide range of learning object repositories, most systems provide access to a single learning object repository.
- *Location.* Recommendations are usually produced at recommendation server. Fewer systems produce them at the information source. Recent research on recommender systems is increasingly oriented to produce recommendations on the

Table 3.5 Classification of TEL recommenders, according to Personalisation characteristics

Approach: Personalisation			
Method		Collaborative filtering	[RS1], [RS3], [RS4], [RS5], [RS9], [RS10], [RS11], [RS13], [RS18], [RS25], [RS27], [RS31], [RS38], [RS39], [RS42]
		Content-based	[RS16], [RS27], [RS29], [RS30], [RS32], [RS38]
		Hybrid	[RS8], [RS14], [RS20], [RS34], [RS38], [RS41]
		Rule-based	[RS6], [RS21], [RS22], [RS23], [RS24], [RS28], [RS33], [RS36], [RS37], [RS40]
Algorithm	Type	Model-based	[RS20], [RS21], [RS22], [RS23], [RS27], [RS28], [RS29], [RS30], [RS32], [RS35], [RS36], [RS37], [RS40]
		Memory-based	[RS1], [RS3], [RS4], [RS5], [RS9], [RS11], [RS14], [RS18], [RS25], [RS27], [RS39], [RS42]
		Hybrid	[RS10], [RS24], [RS34], [RS38], [RS41]
	Technique	Attribute-based	[RS10], [RS16], [RS29]
		Item-to-item	[RS25], [RS27], [RS42]
		User-to-user	[RS1], [RS3], [RS4], [RS9], [RS11], [RS27], [RS31], [RS39]
		Hybrid	[RS13], [RS14], [RS20], [RS34], [RS37], [RS38]
		Vector-space model	[RS30], [RS32]
Output		Suggestion	[RS1], [RS4], [RS5], [RS6], [RS8], [RS13], [RS14], [RS16], [RS18], [RS21], [RS22], [RS23], [RS24], [RS25], [RS28], [RS29], [RS30], [RS32], [RS33], [RS34], [RS36], [RS37], [RS38], [RS40], [RS41]
		Prediction	[RS2], [RS9], [RS27], [RS31], [RS35], [RS39], [RS42]

user side—i.e. for use on mobile devices in situated learning activities. Ongoing work in this area has been described in (Verbert et al. to appear).

- *Mode*. Until now, TEL recommender systems either provide their recommendations at an active 'Pull mode' where users request relevant recommendations or in a 'Passive' mode where users receive recommendations as part of their natural interaction with the system. None of the systems we reviewed automatically sends recommendations to the user with 'Push mode'. CYCLADES **[RS4]** (Avancini and Straccia 2005) is an example of a system that also supports a 'Passive mode'

Table 3.6 Classification of TEL recommenders, according to the Domain Model of the Approach category

Operation		
Architecture	Centralised	[RS1], [RS2], [RS3], [RS5], [RS6], [RS8], [RS9], [RS11], [RS13], [RS14], [RS16], [RS18], [RS19], [RS23], [RS24], [RS25], [RS27], [RS28], [RS29], [RS31], [RS33], [RS35], [RS36], [RS37], [RS38], [RS39], [RS40], [RS41], [RS42]
	Distributed	[RS4], [RS20], [RS21], [RS22], [RS30], [RS32], [RS34]
Location	At information source	[RS2], [RS9], [RS27], [RS31], [RS35], [RS39]
	At recommendation server	[RS3], [RS4], [RS5], [RS6], [RS8], [RS13], [RS14], [RS16], [RS18], [RS19], [RS20], [RS21], [RS22], [RS23], [RS25], [RS27], [RS28], [RS29], [RS30], [RS31], [RS32], [RS33], [RS34], [RS35], [RS36], [RS37], [RS38], [RS39], [RS40], [RS41], [RS42]
Mode	Pull (active)	[RS1], [RS3], [RS4], [RS5], [RS9], [RS14], [RS26], [RS29], [RS32], [RS35], [RS41], [RS42]
	Passive	[RS4], [RS8], [RS13], [RS16], [RS20], [RS22], [RS23], [RS25], [RS28], [RS33], [RS34], [RS36], [RS37], [RS40]

and produces recommendations as part of the natural interaction of the user with the system—without explicit requests for recommendations.

3.2.3 Conclusions

In this chapter, we used an existing framework for the analysis of recommender systems which we extended slightly in order to support TEL-relevant recommendation tasks, and we performed a review and analysis of a sample of 42 recommendation concepts, prototypes and deployed systems that have been proposed as appropriate for educational applications in the literature. Our analysis indicated that the increased interest in TEL recommenders has led to some very interesting research and development work, which is also experimentally tested either in lab settings or with real users. Existing systems adopt most of the methods and techniques that one can find in recommender systems of other domains, with some preference in algorithmic contributions. It is interesting to note that real-life deployment of such systems is reported to be limited, which inhibits experimental studies focusing on user acceptance and adoption in real learning settings.

This comprehensive analysis of such a large sample that spans over 10 years of relevant work helped us identify some important and pressing challenges in this domain, which are discussed in the following chapter. The literature covered by this analysis, as well as additional references that are contributed after the writing of this chapter, may be found by interested readers in a dedicated group on 'Recommender Systems for Learning' that was created in Mendeley.[3]

References

G. Adomavicius, A. Tuzhilin, Towards the next generation of recommender systems: a survey of the state-of-the-art and possible extensions. IEEE Trans. Knowl. Data Eng. **17**(6), 734–749 (2005)

M. Aehnelt, M. Ebert, G. Beham, S. Lindstaedt, A. Paschen, *A Socio-Technical Approach Towards Supporting Intra-Organizational Collaboration*, ed. by P. Dillenbourg, M. Specht. Times of convergence: technologies across learning contexts. Proceedings of the 3rd European Conference on Technology Enhanced Learning (EC-TEL 2008), Maastricht, The Netherlands, LNCS 5192 (Springer, Berlin, 2008), pp. 33–38

M. Anderson, M. Ball, H. Boley, S. Greene, N. Howse, D. Lemire, S. McGrath, RACOFI: A Rule-Applying Collaborative Filtering System. Paper presented at the conference IEEE/WIC COLA 2003, 13 October 2003, Halifax, Canada. http://www.daniel-lemire.com/fr/abstracts/COLA2003.html. Accessed 11 January 2010

H. Avancini, U. Straccia, User recommendation for collaborative and personalised digital archives. Int. J. Web Based Commun. **1**(2), 163–175 (2005)

G. Beham, B. Kump, T. Ley, S. Lindstaedt, Recommending knowledgeable people in a work-integrated learning system. Procedia Comput. Sci. **1**(2), 2783–2792 (2010)

C. Bodea, M. Dascalu, A. Lipai, in *Clustering of the Web Search Results in Educational Recommender Systems*, ed. by O. Santos, J. Boticario. Educational Recommender Systems and Technologies: Practices and Challenges (IGI Global, Hershey, 2012), pp. 154–181. doi:10.4018/978-1-61350-489-5.ch007

J. Broisin, M. Brut, V. Butoianu, F. Sedes, P. Vidal, A personalised recommendation framework based on CAM and document annotations. Procedia Comput. Sci. **1**(2), 2839–2848 (2010) doi: 10.4018/978-1-61350-489-5.ch007

P. Brusilovsky, Methods and techniques of adaptive hypermedia. User Model. User-Adapt. Interact. **6**(2–3), 87–129 (1996)

P. Brusilovsky, L.N. Cassel, L.M.L. Delcambre, E.A. Fox, R. Furuta, D.D. Garcia, F.M. Shipman III, M. Yudelson, Social navigation for educational digital libraries. Procedia Comput. Sci. **1**(2), 2889–2897 (2010)

R. Burke, Hybrid recommender systems: survey and experiments. User Model. User Adapt. Interact. **12**, 331–370 (2002)

A. Casali, V. Gerling, C. Deco, C. Bender, *A Recommender System for Learning Objects Personalized Retrieval*, ed. by O. Santos, J. Boticario. Educational Recommender Systems and Technologies: Practices and Challenges (IGI Global, Hershey, 2012), pp. 182–210. doi: 10.4018/978-1-61350-489-5.ch008

A. Diaz, R. Motz, E. Rohrer, L. Tansini, *An Ontology Network for Educational Recommender Systems*, ed. by O. Santos, J. Boticario. Educational Recommender Systems and Technologies: Practices and Challenges (IGI Global, Hershey, 2012), pp. 67–93. doi: 10.4018/978-1-61350-489-5.ch004

---

[3] http://www.mendeley.com/groups/1969281/recommender-systems-for-learning/

H. Drachsler, D. Pecceu, T. Arts, E. Hutten, L. Rutledge, P. Van Rosmalen, H.G.K. Hummel, R. Koper, *ReMashed-Recommendations for Mash-Up Personal Learning Environments*, ed. by U. Cress, V. Dimitrova, M. Specht. Learning in the Synergy of Multiple Disciplines, Proceedings of the 4th European Conference on Technology Enhanced Learning (EC-TEL 2009), LNCS 5794 (Springer, Berlin, 2009a), pp. 788–793

H. Drachsler, D. Pecceu, T. Arts, E. Hutten, L. Rutledge, P. Van Rosmalen, H.G.K. Hummel, R. Koper, in *ReMashed-An Usability Study of a Recommender System for Mash-Ups for Learning*. 1st Workshop on Mashups for Learning at the International Conference on Interactive Computer Aided Learning, Villach, Austria, 2009b

H. Drachsler, H.G.K. Hummel, B. Van den Berg, J. Eshuis, A. Berlanga, R. Nadolski, W. Waterink, N. Boers, R. Koper, Effects of the ISIS recommender system for navigation support in self-organized learning networks. Educ. Technol. Soc. **12**, 122–135 (2009c)

H. Drachsler, W. Greller, in *The Pulse of Learning Analytics—Understandings and Expectations from the Stakeholders*. Proceedings of the 2nd Learning Analytics Conference, Vancouver, Canada, April 2012

J. Dron, R. Mitchell, C. Boyne, P. Siviter, in *CoFIND: steps towards a self-organising learning environment*. Proceedings of the World Conference on the WWW and Internet (WebNet 2000), San Antonio, Texas, USA, October 30–November 4, 2000a, pp. 146–151. AACE, USA

J. Dron, R. Mitchell, P. Siviter, C. Boyne, CoFIND-an experiment in n-dimensional collaborative filtering. J. Netw. Comput. Appl. **23**(2), 131–142 (2000b)

S. El Helou, C. Salzmann, D. Gillet, The 3A personalised, contextual and relation-based recommender system. J. Univers. Comput. Sci. **16**(16), 2179–2195 (2010)

R. Farzan, P. Brusilovsky, Encouraging user participation in a course recommender system: an impact on user behavior. Comput. Human Behav. **27**(1), 276–284 (2010)

J. Fiaidhi, RecoSearch: a model for collaboratively filtering java learning objects. Int. J. Instr. Technol. Distance Learn. **1**(7), 35–50 (2004)

M. Friedrich, M. Wolpers, R. Shen, C. Ullrich, R. Klamma, D. Renzel, A. Richert, B. von der Heiden, Early results of experiments with responsive open learning environments. J. Univers. Comput. Sci. **17**(3), 451–471 (2011)

M. Gomez-Albarran, G. Jimenez-Diaz, Recommendation and students' authoring in repositories of learning objects: a case-based reasoning approach. Int. J. Emerg. Technol. Learn. (iJET) **4**(1), 35–40 (2009)

P. Han, B. Xie, F. Yang, R. Shen, A scalable P2P recommender system based on distributed collaborative filtering. Expert Syst. Appl. **27**, 203–210 (2004)

U. Hanani, B. Shapira, P. Shoval, Information filtering: overview of issues, research and systems. User Model. User-Adapt. Interact. **11**, 203–259 (2001)

J.L. Herlocker, J.A. Konstan, L.G. Terveen, J.T. Riedl, Evaluating collaborative filtering recommender systems. ACM Trans. Inf. Syst. **22**(1), 5–53 (2004)

Y.-M. Huang, T.-C. Huang, K.-T. Wang, W.-Y. Hwang, A Markov-based recommendation model for exploring the transfer of learning on the web. Educ. Technol. Soc. **12**(2), 144–162 (2009)

H.G.K. Hummel, B. Van den Berg, A.J. Berlanga, H. Drachsler, J. Janssen, R.J. Nadolski, R. Koper, Combining social- and information-based approaches for personalised recommendation on sequencing learning activities. Int. J. Learn. Technol. **3**(2), 152–168 (2007)

J. Janssen, C. Tattersall, W. Waterink, B. Van den Berg, R. Van Es, C. Bolman, Self-organising navigational support in lifelong learning: how predecessors can lead the way. Comput. Educ. **49**(3), 781–793 (2005)

M.K. Khribi, M. Jemni, O. Nasraoui, Automatic recommendations for e-learning personalization based on web usage mining techniques and information retrieval. Educ. Technol. Soc. **12**(4), 30–42 (2009)

R. Klamma, M. Spaniol, Y. Cao, in *Community Aware Content Adaptation for Mobile Technology Enhanced Learning*. Innovative Approaches for Learning and Knowledge Sharing, 2006, pp. 227–241

R. Koper, Increasing learner retention in a simulated learning network using indirect social interaction. J. Artif. Soc. Soc. Simul. **8**(2) (2005). http://jasss.soc.surrey.ac.uk/8/2/5.html

G. Koutrika, R. Ikeda, B. Bercovitz, H. Garcia-Molina, in *Flexible Recommendations over Rich Data*. Proceedings of the 2nd ACM International Conference on Recommender Systems (RecSys'08), Lausanne, Switzerland, 2008

G. Koutrika, B. Bercovitz, F. Kaliszan, H. Liou, H. Garcia-Molina, in *CourseRank: A Closed-Community Social System Through the Magnifying Glass*. Proceedings of the 3rd International AAAI Conference on Weblogs and Social Media (ICWSM'09), San Jose, California, 2009

V. Kumar, J. Nesbit, K. Han, in *Rating Learning Object Quality with Distributed Bayesian Belief Networks: The Why and the How*. Proceedings of the Fifth IEEE International Conference on Advanced Learning Technologies, ICALT'05, 2005

C. Lagoze, H. Van de Sompel, in *The open archives initiative: building a low-barrier interoperability framework*. Proceedings of the 1st ACM/IEEE-CS Joint Conference on Digital Libraries (JCDL '01), (ACM, New York, NY, USA, 2001), pp. 54–62

D. Lemire, Scale and translation invariant collaborative filtering systems. J. Inf. Retr. **8**(1), 129–150 (2005)

D. Lemire, H. Boley, S. McGrath, M. Ball, Collaborative filtering and inference rules for context-aware learning object recommendation. Int. J. Interact. Technol. Smart Educ. **2**(3), 179–188 (2005)

N. Manouselis, C. Costopoulou, Analysis and Classification of Multi-Criteria Recommender Systems. World Wide Web: Internet and Web Information Systems, Special Issue on Multi-channel Adaptive Information Systems on the World Wide Web **10**(4), 415–441 (2007a)

N. Manouselis, C. Costopoulou, Experimental analysis of design choices in multi-attribute utility collaborative filtering. Int. J. Pattern Recognit. Art. Intell. (Special Issue on Personalization Techniques for Recommender Systems and Intelligent User Interfaces) **21**(2), 311–333 (2007b)

N. Manouselis, R. Vuorikari, F. Van Assche, in *Simulated Analysis of MAUT Collaborative Filtering for Learning Object Recommendation*. Proceedings of the Workshop on Social Information Retrieval in Technology Enhanced Learning (SIRTEL 2007), Crete, Greece, 2007

N. Manouselis, R. Vuorikari, F. Van Assche, Collaborative recommendation of e-learning resources: an experimental investigation. J. Comput. Assist. Learn. (Special Issue on Adaptive technologies and methods in e/m-Learning and Internet-based education, Blackwell Publishing Ltd.) **26**(4), 227–242 (2010)

L.B. Marinho, A. Nanopoulos, L. Schmidt-Thieme, R. Jäschke, A. Hotho, G. Stumme, P. Symeonidis, in *Social Tagging Recommender Systems*, ed. by P. Kantor, F. Ricci, L. Rokach, B. Shapira. 1st Recommender Systems Handbook: A Complete Guide for Research Scientists and Practitioners (Springer, Berlin, 2010)

O. Marino, G. Paquette, A competency-driven advisor system for multi-actor learning environments. Procedia Comput. Sci. **1**(2), 2871–2876 (2010). doi: 10.1016/j.procs.2010.08.013

P. Michlik, M. Bielikova, Exercises recommending for limited time learning. Procedia Comput. Sci. **1**(2), 2821–2828 (2010) doi: 10.1016/j.procs.2010.08.007

B.N. Miller, J.A. Konstan, J. Riedl, PocketLens: toward a personal recommender system. ACM Trans. Inf. Syst. **22**(3), 437–476 (2004)

F. Moedritscher, Towards a recommender strategy for personal learning environments. Procedia Comput. Sci. **1**(2), 2775–2782 (2010). doi: 10.1016/j.procs.2010.08.002

M. Montaner, B. Lopez, J.L. de la Rosa, A taxonomy of recommender agents on the internet. Artif. Intell. Rev. **19**, 285–330 (2003)

R.J. Nadolski, B. Van den Berg, A. Berlanga, H. Drachsler, H. Hummel, R. Koper, P. Sloep, Simulating light-weight personalised recommender systems in learning networks: a case for pedagogy-oriented and rating-based hybrid recommendation strategies. J. Artif. Soc. Social Simul. (JASSS) **12**(14) (2009). http://jasss.soc.surrey.ac.uk/12/1/4.html

I. Okoye, K. Maull, J. Foster, T. Sumner, in *Educational Recommendation in an Informal Intentional Learning System*, ed. by O. Santos, J. Boticario, Educational Recommender Systems and

Technologies: Practices and Challenges (IGI Global, Hershey, 2012), pp. 1–23. doi: 10.4018/ 978-1-61350-489-5.ch001

S. Rafaeli, M. Barak, Y. Dan-Gur, E. Toch, QSIA-a Web-based environment for learning, assessing and knowledge sharing in communities. Comput. Educ. **43**(3), 273–289 (2004)

S. Rafaeli, Y. Dan-Gur, M. Barak, Social recommender systems: recommendations in support of e-learning. Int. J. Distance Educ. Technol. **3**(2), 29–45 (2005)

M.M. Recker, A. Walker, Supporting "Word-of-Mouth" social networks through collaborative information filtering. J. Interact. Learn. Res. **14**(1), 79–99 (2003)

M.M. Recker, D.A. Wiley, A non-authoritative educational metadata ontology for filtering and recommending learning objects. Interact. Learn. Environ. **9**(3), 255–271 (2001)

M.M. Recker, A. Walker, D. Wiley, in *An interface for collaborative filtering of educational resources*. International Conference on Artificial Intelligence, Las Vegas, Nevada, USA, 2000, pp. 26–29

M.M. Recker, A. Walker, K. Lawless, What do you recommend? Implementation and analyses of collaborative information filtering of web resources for education. Instr. Sci. **31**(4/5), 299–316 (2003)

O.C. Santos, in *A recommender system to provide adaptive and inclusive standard-based support along the eLearning life cycle*. Proceedings of the 2008 ACM conference on Recommender systems, (ACM, 2008), pp. 319–322

J.B. Schafer, J.A. Konstan, J. Riedl, E-commerce recommendation applications. Data Min. Knowl. Discov. **5**, 115–153 (2001)

K. Schoefegger, P. Seitlinger, T. Ley, Towards a user model for personalised recommendations in work-integrated learning: a report on an experimental study with a collaborative tagging system. Procedia Comput. Sci. **1**(2), 2829–2838 (2010) doi: 10.1016/j.procs.2010.05.008

B.E. Shelton, J. Duffin, Y. Wang, J. Ball, Linking open course wares and open education resources: creating an effective search and recommendation system. Procedia Comput. Sci. **1**(2), 2865–2870 (2010) doi: 10.1016/j.procs.2010.08.012

L. Shen, R. Shen, in *Learning Content Recommendation Service Based-On Simple Sequencing Specification*, ed. by W. Liu et al. (eds). Lecture notes in computer science (Springer, Berlin, 2004), pp. 363–370

M.A. Sicilia, E. Garca-Barriocanal, S. Snchez-Alonso, C. Cechinel, Exploring user-based recommender results in large learning object repositories: the case of MERLOT. Procedia Comput. Sci. **1**(2), 2859–2864 (2010) doi: 10.1016/j.procs.2010.08.011

R. Sie, H. Drachsler, M. Bitter, P. Sloep, To whom and why should I connect? Co-author recommendation based on powerful and similar peers. Int. J. Technol. Enhanc. Learn. (to appear)

G.A. Sielis, C. Mettouris, A. Tzanavari, G.A. Papadopoulos, in *Context-aware recommendations using topic maps technology for the enhancement of the creativity process*, ed. by O. Santos, J. Boticario. Educational Recommender Systems and Technologies: Practices and Challenges (IGI Global, Hershey, 2012), pp. 43–66. doi: 10.4018/978-1-61350-489-5.ch003

J. Stamper, EDM and the 4th paradigm of scientific discovery. https://pslcdatashop.web.cmu.edu/ about/edm_stamper_2011.html. Accessed 1 August 2011

T. Tang, G. McCalla, in *Smart Recommendation for an Evolving E-Learning System*. Proceedings of the Workshop on Technologies for Electronic Documents for Supporting Learning, International Conference on Artificial Intelligence in Education (AIED 2003), 2003, pp. 699–710

T. Tang, G. McCalla, in *Utilizing Artificial Learner on the Cold-Start Pedagogical-Value based Paper Recommendation*. Proceedings of AH 2004: International Conference on Adaptive Hypermedia and Adaptive Web-Based Systems, 2004

T. Tang, G. McCalla, in *Beyond Learners' Interest: Personalized Paper Recommendation Based on Their Pedagogical Features for an e-Learning System*. Proceedings of the 8th Pacific Rim International Conference on Artificial Intelligence (PRICAI 2004), 2004, pp. 301–310

T.Y. Tang, G. McCalla, in *On the pedagogically guided paper recommendation for an evolving web-based learning system*. Proceedings of the 17th International FLAIRS Conference, 2004, pp. 86–91

T.Y. Tang, G. McCalla, Smart recommendation for an evolving e-learning system: architecture and experiment. Int. J. E-Learn. **4**(1), 105–129 (2005)

N. Thai-Nghe, L. Drumond, T. Horvth, A. Krohn-Grimberghe, A. Nanopoulos, L. Schmidt-Thieme, in *Factorization Techniques for Predicting Student Performance*, ed. by O. Santos, J. Boticario. Educational Recommender Systems and Technologies: Practices and Challenges (IGI Global, Hershey, 2012), pp. 129–153. doi: 10.4018/978-1-61350-489-5.ch006

N. Thai-Nghe, L. Drumond, A. Krohn-Grimberghe, L. Schmidt-Thieme, Recommender system for predicting student performance. Procedia Comput. Sci. **1**(2), 2811–2819 (2010) doi: 10.1016/j.procs.2010.08.006

K.H. Tsai, T.K. Chiu, M.C. Lee, T.I. Wang, in *A learning objects recommendation model based on the preference and ontological approaches*. Proceedings of 6th International Conference on Advanced Learning Technologies (ICALT'06) (IEEE Computer Society Press, New York, 2006)

J.S. Underwood, in *Metis: A Content Map-Based Recommender System for Digital Learning Activities*, ed. by O. Santos, J. Boticario. Educational Recommender Systems and Technologies: Practices and Challenges (IGI Global, Hershey, 2012), pp. 24–42. doi: 10.4018/978-1-61350-489-5.ch002

M. Van Setten, Supporting people in finding information: hybrid recommender systems and goal-based structuring. Telematica Instituut Fundamental Research Series NO. 016 (TI/FRS/016), 2005, Enschede, The Netherlands

K. Verbert, H. Drachsler, N. Manouselis, M. Wolpers, R. Vuorikari, E. Duval, *Dataset-driven research for improving recommender systems for learning*. Proceedings of the 1st International Conference on Learning Analytics and Knowledge (ACM, New York, NY, USA, 2011), pp. 44–53

K. Verbert, N. Manouselis, O. Xavier, M. Wolpers, H. Drachsler, I. Bosnic, E. Duval, Context-aware recommender systems for learning: a survey and future challenges. IEEE Trans. Learn. Technol. https://lirias.kuleuven.be/handle/123456789/338644, to appear

L.S. Vygotsky, *Mind in Society: The Development of Higher Psychological Processes* (Harvard University Press, Cambridge, 1978)

A. Walker, M. Recker, K. Lawless, D. Wiley, Collaborative information filtering: a review and an educational application. Int. J. Artif. Intell. Educ. **14**(1), 3–28 (2004)

Y. Wang, K. Sumiya, Semantic ranking of lecture slides based on conceptual relationship and presentational structure. Procedia Comput. Sci. **1**(2), 2801–2810 (2010) doi: 10.1016/j.procs.2010.08.005

C.-P. Wei, M.J. Shaw, R.F. Easley, in *A Survey of Recommendation Systems in Electronic Commerce*, ed. by R.T. Rust, P.K. Kannan. New Directions in Theory and Practice (M. E. Sharpe Publisher, E-Serv, Armonk, 2002)

V.A.R. Zaldivar, D. Burgos, Meta-mender: a meta-rule based recommendation system for educational applications. Procedia Comput. Sci. **1**(2), 2877–2882 (2010). doi: 10.1016/j.procs.2010.08.014

V.A. Zaldivar, D. Burgos, A. Pardo, in *Meta-Rule Based Recommender Systems for Educational Applications*, ed. by O. Santos, J. Boticario, Educational Recommender Systems and Technologies: Practices and Challenges (IGI Global, Hershey, 2012), pp. 211–231. doi: 10.4018/978-1-61350-489-5.ch009

M. Zhou, Y. Xu, in *Challenges to Use Recommender Systems to Enhance Meta-Cognitive Functioning in Online Learners*, ed. by O. Santos, J. Boticario, Educational Recommender Systems and Technologies: Practices and Challenges (IGI Global, Hershey, 2012) pp. 282–301. doi: 10.4018/978-1-61350-489-5.ch012

Chapter 4
Challenges and Outlook

Abstract This chapter discusses the main challenges that we see as being highlighted from this study. It also outlines the directions of future work that relevant research could take. It concludes with the main contributions and lessons learnt of this work.

4.1 Challenges for TEL Recommendation

In Chap. 2, we introduced some recommendation tasks that systems may support in educational settings coming from the general literature of recommender systems (Herlocker et al. 2004), as well as suggested some recommendation tasks that are particularly relevant in education. Nevertheless, matching the appropriate recommendation approach or technology to the educational domain is not a straight-forward task. Some heuristics for selecting an appropriate technology have been recently proposed by Burke and Ramezani (2011). They described targeted domains using a number of attributes such as:

- How heterogeneous the item space is: that is, if it encompasses many items with different characteristics that may satisfy different goals.
- The degree of risk that a user incurs in accepting a recommendation: that is, if there is tolerance to false recommendations and their implications.
- The time span of the items: that is, how often and in which ways do items appear and then disappear from the domain.
- How the user input is collected: that is, the way, type and format in which user preferences are usually expressed.
- The evolution and temporal stability of the user model: that is, how frequent are user preference data being collected and updated, and the degree in which temporal restrictions apply to the recommendation.

N. Manouselis et al., *Recommender Systems for Learning*,
SpringerBriefs in Electrical and Computer Engineering,
DOI: 10.1007/978-1-4614-4361-2_4, © The Authors 2013

- If recommendations need to be justified: that is, if the domain requires recommendations that need to be credible and explainable or there is some degree of tolerance and explanations are not needed.

Concluding the above mentioned aspects, recommender system designers need to carefully analyse their recommendation tasks and have a representative data set of the target domain and the users available in order to provide valuable and accurate recommendations in TEL. One could argue that in recommender systems for teaching and learning, most of these attributes can be specified and explored, so that appropriate recommendation tasks, techniques, and models can be pre-assessed and selected. As a matter of fact, earlier work from Drachsler et al. (2008) has already discussed the appropriateness and usefulness of various recommendation techniques for TEL. But predicting and recommending suitable resources for learning processes still remains more complex than predicting a certain consumer behaviour. In the following sections, we describe a number of research challenges that have already been identified in relevant literature or seem to be emerging in this domain.

4.1.1 Pedagogy and Cognition

Recent work on the social and psychological requirements on how people react to and act upon recommender systems for the learning sciences has shed some new insights into the pedagogical discussion (Howard-Jones et al. 2010). More specifically, Buder and Schwind (2012) have studied a conceptualisation that departs from initial work in e-commerce recommendation (Xiao and Benbasat 2007). They focus on how learners deal with recommended items as well as being the data producers that serve the computation of the system by contributing annotations, tags or ratings. In their approach, a number of important principles need to be considered to fit recommender systems in the educational domain:

- Recommender systems shift responsibility away from dedicated experts.
- The quality of the content is not traceable to any individual output but rather to the community's collective behaviour.
- Recommender systems provide (and require) user control thus facilitating self-regulated learning.
- Recommender systems provide guidance to learning activities.
- Recommender systems adapt to the needs and requirements of learners.

Most of the mentioned principles are addressed by today's TEL recommender systems. But Buder and Schwind (2012) emphasised that there are too few educational and psychological studies about the effects of recommender systems on different learners (specific preferences, formal vs. informal learning), learning tasks, or knowledge levels like conducted by Janssen et al. (2005) or Drachsler et al. (2009). Furthermore, they suggest selecting recommendation strategies according to the roles that the users are expected to play. They define new educational requirements that emphasise the need for context-awareness with regard to knowledge and activities, persuasiveness and critical thinking, participation and meta-cognitive stimulation, as well as increasing the explicit expression of learner preferences through direct or indirect ratings. Context-awareness and support of meta-cognitive process are well known as critical criteria to provide meaningful recommendations in TEL. Many of the systems that aim to support competence development of learners take those aspects into account (e.g. Zaldivar and Burgos 2010; Okoye et al. 2012; Drachsler et al. 2009; Thai-Nghe et al. 2010). Verbert et al. (to appearB) published a comprehensive overview of relevant context variables for TEL recommender systems.

Zhou and Xu (2012) also emphasised the educational requirement to support meta-cognitive activities of learners with recommender systems. In order to improve the learning process, recommender systems should be able to guide learners and recommend learning activities or strategies to support monitoring, reflection, and control of the individual learning goals. Zhou and Xu (2012) identify the following five considerations that TEL recommenders need to take into account to address meta-cognitive processes:

• Consider both learner attributes and the learning sequences during recommendations.
• Detect meaningful learning activities and translate them into a learning strategy.
• Recommend learning activities based on multiple features instead of recommending static learning resources.
• Retrieve learner preferences (learning goals, tasks, and contexts) from a learner profile and adapt learning strategies according to the learner's progress and performance at different learning stages.
• Detect the learners' motivation and their changes during the learning process to recommend suitable learning strategies.

The first four considerations (learner attributes, recommend sequences, detect meaningful activities, use multiple features) are already addressed by current research. Nevertheless, there is further research needed to find most effective solutions for specific learning settings and to create a transparent overview of the effects of different recommendation approaches. Other considerations like the motivation detection seem to be quite challenging and still to be explored. Both Zhou and Xu (2012) and Buder and Schwind (2012) point out that many of these requirements are suggested based on speculation; nevertheless they draw a picture of the overall expectations from the educational field towards educational recommender systems. They emphasise what Drachsler et al. already outlined in 2008, recommender systems in TEL should aim higher than just recommending learning resources like movies, they should actively support the learner in the learning process. This unsolved challenge requires two additional aspects: (a) additional data sources that also track e.g. motional patterns of users; (b) the application of data mining techniques to create more comprehensive learner models. With respect to (a), interesting research opportunities are emerging with the Neuro-Educational research field (Howard-Jones 2010). Today, we can make technology adapt dynamically to changing needs of learners based activity traces and expressed interests. This information can be extended in the future by neuroscience data and taken into account by adaptive educational systems and recommender systems. Neuro-Educational research has been highlighted in the UK as an area of research deserving future investment (Royal Society 2011). The same applies for (b) with the EDM and the emerging LAK research fields. However, until now, little work has focused specifically on the potential of the neurosciences data to create learner models for educational recommendations.

4.1.2 Evaluation

Typically, evaluation of recommender systems covers three types of experiments that are motivated by evaluation protocols in areas such as information retrieval (Shani and Gunawardana 2011):

- Offline experiments, using pre-collected or simulated data to test the performance of candidate algorithms;
- User studies, where a small group of subjects use a system in a controlled environment and report on their experience;
- Real life testing, where a system is tested under realistic conditions during its normal operation with its actual users.

As reported in Chap. 3, until today evaluation of TEL recommender systems mostly takes place in the form of offline experiments as well as the conduction of controlled user studies. Real life testing of systems in an educational context and over a larger time span that will allow the measurement of their actual acceptance, usage and effect on the learners, still needs further work.

As far as offline experiments are concerned, they mostly follow the typical approach of similar recommendation algorithm testing in other domains (Herlocker et al. 2004; Shani and Gunawardana 2011). Studies such as the experiments of Lemire et al. (2005), Manouselis et al. (2010), Sicilia et al. (2010) and Verbert et al. (2011) adopt and showcase this approach, using data sets from educational applications and environments. Related work in TEL recommenders can follow the settings and protocols that already flourish in relevant literature and rather focus on the data sets that they can use for experimentation, as it is discussed in Sect. 4.1.3 later on.

Controlled user studies are very valuable and often used in educational settings. Typical studies are the ones of Dron et al. (2000), Recker et al. (2003), and Drachsler et al. (2009). They can also contribute to evaluate specific technological aspects of the system, apart from empirical evidences of psychological and pedagogical aspects that can be collected through such controlled experiments. A common problem is the 'monolithic' evaluation of adaptive systems, when the adaptation process is treated as a whole entity instead of depended levels of adaptation (Brusilovsky and Eklund 1998). This 'monolithic' cannot provide results at a level of granularity that can be of practical use and help the system designer to decide which part of the system needs improvement (e.g. the user modelling, the domain modelling, the recommendation technique).

An interesting approach has been proposed by Brusilovsky et al. (2001): to decompose the adaptation process into two layers that are evaluated separately. The main idea behind the approach was that the evaluation of adaptive systems should not treat adaptation as a monolithic/singular process happening behind the scenes. Rather, adaptation should be broken down into its constituents, and each of these constituents should be evaluated separately where necessary and feasible (Karagiannidis and Sampson 2000).

Simultaneously with the idea of evaluating adaptation at two different layers (Brusilovsky et al. 2001), two other layered (also referred to as modular) evaluation frameworks have been proposed. The process-based framework presented by Weibelzahl (2001) consisted from four layers that referred to the information processing steps within the adaptation process: evaluation of input data, evaluation of the inference mechanism, evaluation of the adaptation decision, and evaluation of the total interaction. A second framework has been presented by Paramythis et al. (2001) and is more detailed in terms of different components involved in the adaptation process. It also addressed the question of methods and tools appropriate for the evaluation of different adaptation modules to yield input for the development process. A merged version of the two frameworks was finally proposed, identifying both criteria to be taken into consideration in the evaluation of an adaptive system, and the methods and tools that can be engaged to do so (Weibelzahl et al. 2003). This modular evaluation approach has been explored by several studies that evaluate adaptive systems (e.g. Brusilovsky et al. 2004), but to our knowledge, it has not been yet formally developed and applied for recommender systems.

Finally, the realistic evaluation of deployed recommender systems that are supporting some real educational activity has not yet been explored to the desired degree. One step is carrying out experiments that will test various aspects of an operating system with its real users, for instance by employing online testing systems where multiple algorithms can be compared without the users realising that they interact with an alternative recommendation engine (Kohavi et al. 2009; Shani and Gunawardana 2011). A more complete step would be designing and carrying out longer-term experiments (e.g. longitudinal studies) that will go deeper into the way that recommender systems may change the way learners acquire new knowledge and then apply it in a given setting. Traditional approaches could be adapted and followed such as the model of Kirkpatrick (1959) that measures the success of training using four different layers. In a TEL recommendation context, it could be used to explore the following layers:

(a) **Reaction of user**—what they thought and felt (Did the learners enjoy the recommendations they received?);
(b) **Learning**—the resulting increase in gaining new knowledge or capabilities (Did the learners learn what they needed to and get some new ideas, with the help of the recommender?);
(c) **Behaviour**—extent of how acquired knowledge and capability can be implemented/applied in real life (Did the learners use the new information and ideas that they were recommended?);

(d) **Results**—the effects on the user's performance in the learning or working environment (Did the ideas and information that they were recommended improve the learners' effectiveness and results?).

Overall, evaluation of recommender systems in this domain seams to have significant room for further research. Significant methodological contributions would be particularly valuable, such as proposals for evaluation frameworks (Drachsler et al. 2009, 2010) that will include :

- A detailed analysis of the evaluation methods and tools that can be employed for evaluating TEL recommendation techniques against a set of criteria that will be proposed for each of the selected components (e.g. user model, domain model, recommendation strategy and algorithm).
- The specification of evaluation metrics/indicators to measure the success of each component (e.g. evaluating accuracy of the recommendation algorithm, evaluating coverage of the domain model).
- The elaboration of a number of methods and instruments that can be engaged in TEL settings, in order to collect evaluation data from engaged stakeholders, explicitly or implicitly, e.g. measuring user satisfaction, assessing impact of engaging the TEL recommender from improvements in working tasks.

4.1.3 Data Sets

One of the catalysts in the boost of recommender systems in various domains has been the existence of publicly available data sets that the designers and developers of such systems may use to test and compare their approaches. The $1M prize of Netflix for the algorithm that would significantly improve their previous approach received wide publicity and attracted more than 41,000 teams from over 185 countries around the world to submit around 44,000 different algorithms that tried to achieve this improvement (http://www.netflixprize.com). In addition, several data challenges are regularly being organised, attracting researchers to specific topics and applications (Said et al. 2010, 2011).

In 2011, the TEL recommenders community was still working with small home-made data sets which were not made public available (Manouselis et al. 2010, 2011). It was around that time when a dedicated Theme Team of the European network of excellence STELLAR called dataTEL (Drachsler et al. 2010) started a more concrete analysis of issues around the development, sharing and using of TEL data sets for relevant research, which organised the first dataTEL Challenge, a call for TEL data sets that invited research groups to submit existing data sets from TEL applications that can be used as input for TEL recommender systems. This has resulted in attracting seven data sets that were made available for recommender systems' researchers to work with, including the very large 'Mendeley DataTEL data set' (Jack et al. to appear) from the popular social research platform Mendeley.com.

In parallel, the community of Educational Data Mining (EDM) set up its own data set sharing repository (Koedinger et al. 2008) that evolved into the online data analysis service for the learning sciences PSLC dataShop[1] (Koedinger et al. 2010). Other relevant initiatives also emerged, like the Mulce project (Reffay and Betbeder 2009) and LinkedEducation.org. Although these data sets have not specifically been published to facilitate recommender systems' research, they could be used as experimental data for research and testing purposes. In this way, as presented in Chap. 2 and discussed in relevant work, the availability of data sets that could be made available for experimentation has become significantly higher, with more than 20 data sets cited in relevant literature (Verbert et al. 2011, to appearA).

Still, there are several issues that need to be resolved before the uptake and usage of such data sets can become standard practice as in other domains (Ekstrand et al. 2011). Education will not benefit from simple 'users vs. items' rating matrices, and the corresponding data sets will need to be significantly more complex and rich in information. Furthermore, privacy rights and licensing of educational data is a crucial issue. Although an enormous amount of data has been captured from learning environments, it is a difficult process to make these data available for research purposes. The issue of usage privacy rights / licensing needs to be solved from two perspectives. From a user perspective, learners need to be informed and grant permission to collect their data and make it available for research purposes. Also the organisation or provider of these data needs to agree with collecting and sharing these data. For instance, researchers have in some cases collected data sets by crawling data from websites and then found out that they were not allowed to do so. Moreover, the lack of a standard representation for interaction data within data sets prevents the sharing and reuse of data across systems. When a custom data format is not well documented, it may be difficult to assess the meaning and usefulness of data elements that are stored. Finally, the emergence of several Linked Open Data initiatives and efforts in the domain of education (e.g. LinkedEducation.org) and the ongoing publication of information related to educational offerings, services and resources by institutions such as Open University of UK,[2] the National Research Council of Italy,[3] the University of Southampton in UK,[4] the mEducator EU project[5] is also resulting to the availability of new formats, schemas and TEL data sets.[6] We are expecting such developments to further facilitate the experimentation of TEL researchers with relevant data in order to build better recommender systems for the domain. This can be particularly flourishing through research activities and events that bring closer the groups publishing open data and the groups analyzing them, such as the Workshop on Learning Analytics and Linked Data (Drachsler et al. 2012).

---

[1] http://pslcdatashop.org

[2] http://data.open.ac.uk

[3] http://data.cnr.it

[4] http://data.southampton.ac.uk

[5] http://thedatahub.org/dataset/meducator

[6] http://linkeduniversities.org/lu/

4.1.4 Context

As learning is taking place in extremely diverse and rich environments, the incorporation of contextual information about the user in the recommendation process has attracted major interest. Such contextualisation is researched as a paradigm for building intelligent systems that can better predict and anticipate the needs of users, and act more efficiently in response to their behaviour. Algorithms underlying regular recommender systems are not directly transferable to the domain of education. TEL in particular offers some specific characteristics that are not met by today's general purpose recommendation approaches.

One main difference is, of course, that each learner uses her own tools, methods, paths, collaborations and processes. Consequently, guidance within the learning process must be personalised to an extreme extent. Furthermore, learning activities take place in learning environments that are composed of numerous tools and systems. For example, learning management systems (LMSs) provide access to learning resources and collaboration facilities, but do not ensure that teachers or students of a course use them only. Often, learners use additional tools to collaborate or find resources—for instance, in case that the learning material offered in the LMS is not sufficient. Learning situations become even more complex due to the fact that pedagogical approaches differentiate between formal and informal learning processes. Both have different requirements for the learning environment and, as such, for the recommendation within the environment.

The incorporation of additional information about learners and teachers and their context in the recommendation process, becomes of focal interest in this case. Such data can be used to adapt recommendations based on individual learner characteristics, such as learning goals and knowledge levels, and additional contextual information such as available time, location, people nearby, etc. Pioneering work on context-aware recommender systems (CARS) has been done by Adomavicius et al. (2005) and Adomavicius and Tuzhilin (2011). New challenges emerge for capturing and understanding context and exploiting such information for creating intelligent recommendations adapted to current learner needs, without them being necessarily aware of the fact that contextual variables (e.g. the noise or light level) are measured and taken into consideration.

4.1.5 Visualisation

Although recommendation algorithms have been implemented and validated in several promising systems and prototypes as illustrated in Chap. 3, there are important challenges that need to be addressed related to presenting these recommendation to end-users. Among others, people are often confused because they do not understand why certain recommendations are made and why these recommendations change (Schmidt 2007; Lonsdale et al. 2004). As outlined in Herlocker et al. (2000), it is important to explain the rationale behind recommendations to end-users. The complexity of recommendation algorithms often prevents users from comprehending recommended results and can lead to trust issues when recommendations fail.

This complexity is often aggravated by recommendation algorithms that use various types of information in the recommendation process. In addition, recommendation results might change automatically when the context of the user changes. Such automatic updates can be confusing to the user. To deal with this issue, it is important to provide explanations and justify decisions (Ogata and Yano 2004; Abdul-Rahman and Hailes 2000).

An important line of research in this area is the use of visualisation techniques to provide users with insights in the recommendation process. As an example, social visualisations can help to explain recommendation results by explicitly exposing relationships among content and people (Zhao et al. 2010; Klerkx and Duval 2009). El-Bishouty et al. (2007) for instance researched the use of visualisation techniques to present the relationship and distance between recommended peer learners. Such visualisations can be used to easily locate suggested peer learners. Moreover, visualisation techniques can increase understanding of the input and output of a recommender system. Such visualisations can enable the user to meaningfully revise input parameters and thus improve recommendations (Swearingen and Sinha 2001). This objective is particularly important in recommendations that estimate relevant contextual elements based on user behaviour. As the prediction of the current task or interest of the user is a challenging task, there is a need to develop mixed approaches that enable users to provide feedback and help steer this process.

Such research is particularly relevant in a TEL context. Learning success is more difficult to assess than success in e-commerce (item sold) or music (song liked, or volume upped, or song skipped). Explicit relevance feedback in the form of ratings is sparse in the learning domain. Instead, research is increasingly oriented towards the extraction of implicit relevance feedback from actions of users, such as downloads, reading time or tags (Kelly and Belkin 2001). By visualising such data, new patterns and indicators of success may be discovered. These patterns may well span longer sequences of actions than is typically the case in more mainstream recommendation approaches. An added complexity is that learners are not always very good at assessing their own learning results. As such, the combination of visualisation and recommendation techniques to empower users with actionable knowledge to become an active and responsible part-taker in the recommending process, instead of being the typical passive provider of just personal preferences and social connections, is a highly relevant research topic.

4.1.6 Virtualisation

Very large data infrastructures collecting learning content and usage data around it, like the one that Learning Registry[7] is setting up for the USA and Open Discovery

---

[7] http://www.learningregistry.org

Space[8] for Europe, are expected to provide a new perspective into the way that intelligent systems (in general) and recommender systems (in particular) will be developed for TEL. Such infrastructures can help in scaling up TEL recommender systems by allowing them to consume, process and use a rich variety of usage data streams, and thus enable novel forms of real time intelligence that can only become possible on extremely large data volumes.

The existence of global data infrastructures is expected to really stretch the scalability, the robustness and reactivity of today's algorithms and systems, since there is going to be a need to meet a number of upcoming requirements. TEL, as well as other domains, will need to find ways to develop recommender systems that will be able to grow with the volume of data to be handled, to operate at the time scale of the processes they are designed to support and to be able to handle a large variety of data that will be often missing, corrupted or inconsistent.

This also calls for new approaches in the way that recommender systems are going to be developed and running. In a cloud-based environment where execution of services will be distributed, recommendation algorithms will need to be developed as components of an open science Virtual Research Environment like MyExperiment[9] where they will be decomposed to modular workflows of executable components running over virtualised computing resources. Such components, often referred to as 'research objects' (De Roure et al. 2011), may contain raw data, the description of a computational analysis process and the results of executing this process. As De Roure et al. (2011) point out, this offers the capability to reproduce and reuse the research process. In addition, this allows the organisation and development of the various parts of computational processes (such as the different methods used within a recommendation algorithm) as executable components that can be invoked in a standardised way and thus be shared and re-used according to pre-defined protocols and formats. This characteristic makes them appropriate for distribution over virtualised data infrastructures, where cloud and grid computing resources can be used to execute and host different parts of each process, in a way that is invisible to the end user (i.e. the researcher). Since such workflow-based modelling of recommendation algorithms has already started to appear in systems like MyExperiment, and assuming that in the years to come large data infrastructures like Learning Registry and Open Discovery Space will be in place for TEL researchers to use, we expect that this will make significant impact in the way that TEL recommenders are currently being developed, researched and tested.

4.2 Conclusions

In this book, we tried to give a condensed but comprehensive overview of the basic concepts and current applications of recommender systems in the domain of education. We introduced recommender systems and compared them to relevant work

---

[8] http://www.opendiscoveryspace.eu

[9] http://www.myexperiment.org

in TEL like adaptive educational hypermedia, learning networks, educational data mining and learning analytics. Then we emphasised on TEL as a recommendation problem, discussing how the recommendation problem is defined, which the recommendation goals are, and what the recommendation context usually covers as context. We reviewed existing TEL data sets that may be used to support experimentation and testing, as well as discussed about how they can drive relevant research. We reported an extensive analysis of existing recommender systems that can be found in the literature for educational applications. And finally, we reflected on some major challenges that we see as important to be faced in the years to come, also outlining some potential directions of future research. With the presented approach we wanted to stimulate more transparency within the TEL recommender system field. New recommender system approaches could take advantage of the classification presented in this book to position their contribution towards the community efforts and simplify the comparison between different research findings. This would contribute to a more structured body of knowledge of the effects of different recommender systems on various learning settings. Furthermore, the researchers should consider the collected TEL data sets from Chap. 2 as a valuable resource to evaluate their algorithms in the TEL domain.

In an ideal research design, future research efforts will apply four crucial steps for the development and research of TEL recommender systems:

1. A selection of data sets that suit their recommendation problem and tasks.
2. An offline comparison study of different algorithms on the selected data sets.
3. A comprehensive user study in a controlled experimental environment to test psychological, pedagogical and technical aspects of the designed recommender system.
4. A deployment of the recommender system in a real life application, where it can be tested under realistic and normal operational conditions with its actual users.

All these steps need to be accompanied by a good description of the recommendation algorithm tested and selected, the applied user and domain models, and the release of the used data set and other needed data sources to repeat and parameterize any part of the experiment. With such a research design, other TEL researchers could repeat reported experiments, modify user or domain models, or test another recommender algorithm in the same setting to gain comparable and valid results.

References

A. Abdul-Rahman, S. Hailes Supporting trust in virtual communities. in: *Proceedings of the 33rd Annual Hawaii International Conference on System Sciences*, (2000), p. 9

G. Adomavicius, R. Sankaranarayanan, S. Sen, A. Tuzhilin, Incorporating contextual information in recommender systems using a multidimensional approach. ACM Trans. Inform. Syst. (TOIS) **23**(1), 103–145 (2005)

G. Adomavicius, A. Tuzhilin, Context-aware recommender systems. ed *Recommender Systems Handbook*, by F. Ricci, L. Rokach, B. Shapira (Springer, USA, 2011) pp. 217–253

P. Brusilovsky, C. Karagiannidis, D. Sampson, Layered evaluation of adaptive learning systems. Int. J. Continuing Eng. Educ. Lifelong Learn. Spec. Issue Adaptivity Web Mob. Learn. Serv. **14**(4/5), 402–421. (2004), Inderscience Pub

P. Brusilovsky, J. Eklund, A study of user-model based link annotation in educational hypermedia. J. Universal Comput. Sci. Spec. Issue Assess. Issues Educ. Softw. **4**(4), 429–448 (1998)

P. Brusilovsky, C. Karagiannidis, D.G. Sampson, The benefits of layered evaluation of adaptive applications and services. in *Empirical Evaluation of Adaptive Systems. Proceedings of workshop at the Eighth International Conference on User Modeling, UM2001*, ed by S. Weibelzahl, D.N. Chin, G. Weber, (Freiburg, Germany, 2001), p. 8

J. Buder, C. Schwind, Learning with personalized recommender systems: a psychological view. Comput. Hum. Behav. **28**, 207–216 (2012)

R. Burke, M. Ramezani, Matching Recommendation Technologies and Domains, in *Recommender Systems Handbook*, ed by F. Ricci, L. Rokach, B. Shapira (Springer USA, 2011), pp. 367–386

D. De Roure, K. Belhajjam, P. Missier, J.M. Gmez-Prez, R. Palma, J.E. Ruiz, K. Hettne, M. Roos, G. Klyne, C. Goble, Towards the preservation of scientific workflows. in *8th International Conference on Preservation of Digital Objects (iPRES 2011)*, Singapore, 1–4 November 2011

H. Drachsler, H.G.K. Hummel, R. Koper, Personal recommender systems for learners in lifelong learning: requirements, techniques and model. Int. J. Learn. Technol. **3**(4), 404–423 (2008)

H. Drachsler, H.G.K. Hummel, B. Van den Berg, J. Eshuis, A. Berlanga, R. Nadolski, W. Waterink, N. Boers, R. Koper, Effects of the ISIS Recommender System for navigation support in self-organized learning networks. J. Educ. Technol. Soc. **12**, 122–135 (2009)

H. Drachsler, S. Dietze, W. Greller, M. Daquin, J. Jovanovich, A. Pardo, W. Reinhardt, K. Verbert, 1st international workshop on learning analytics and linked data. in *Proceedings of the 2nd Learning Analytics Conference*, (Vancouver, Canada 2012)

H. Drachsler, T. Bogers, R. Vuorikari, K. Verbert, E. Duval, N. Manouselis, G. Beham, S. Lindstaedt, H. Stern, M. Friedrich, Issues and considerations regarding sharable data sets for recommender systems in technology enhanced learning. Procedia Comput. Sci. **1**(2), 2849–2858 (2010). doi:10.1016/j.procs.2010.08.010

J. Dron, R. Mitchell, P. Siviter, C. Boyne, CoFIND-an experiment in n-dimensional collaborative filtering. J. Netw. Comput. Appl. **23**(2), 131–142 (2000)

M.D. Ekstrand, M. Ludwig, J.A. Konstan, J.T. Riedl, Rethinking the recommender research ecosystem: reproducibility, openness, and LensKit. in *Proceedings of the fifth ACM conference on Recommender systems (RecSys '11)*, (ACM, New York. 2011), pp. 133–140

M.M. El-Bishouty, H. Ogata, Y. Yano, Perkam: Personalized knowledge awareness map for computer supported ubiquitous learning. Educ. Technol. Soc. **10**(3), 122–134 (2007)

J.L. Herlocker, J.A. Konstan, L.G. Terveen, J.T. Riedl, Evaluating collaborative filtering recommender systems. ACM Trans. Inform. Syst. **22**(1), 553 (2004)

J.L. Herlocker, J.A. Konstan, J. Riedl, Explaining collaborative filtering recommendations. in *Proceedings of the 2000 ACM conference on Computer supported cooperative work, CSCW 00*, (ACM, New York, 2000), pp. 241–250

P.A. Howard-Jones, *Introducing Neuroeducational Research* (Routledge, Abingdon, 2010)

P. Howard-Jones, M. Ott, T. Van Leeuwen, B. De Smedt, (2010) Neuroscience and technology enhanced learning. ARV White paper. Retrieved from http://www.futurelab.org.uk/resources/neuroscience-and-technology-enhanced-learning

K. Jack, M. Hristakeva, R.G. Zuniga, M. Granitzer, Mendeley's open data for science and learning: a reply to the dataTEL challenge. Int. J. Technol. Enhanced Learn. (to appear)

J. Janssen, C. Tattersall, W. Waterink, B. Van den Berg, R. Van Es, C. Bolman, R. Koper, Self-organising navigational support in lifelong learning: how predecessors can lead the way. Comput. Educ. **49**, 781–793 (2005). http://dx.doi.org/doi:10.1016/j.compedu.2005.11.022

C. Karagiannidis, D.G. Sampson, Layered evaluation of adaptive applications and services. in *Stock Proceedings of International Conference on Adaptive Hypermedia and Adaptive Web-Based Systems, AH2000*, ed by P. Brusilovsky, C.S.O. (Springer, Berlin, 2000), pp. 343346

D. Kelly, N.K. Belkin, Reading time, scrolling and interaction: exploring implicit sources of user preferences for relevance feedback. in *SIGIR01 Proceedings of the 24th Annual International ACM SIGIR Conference on Research and Development in Information Retrieval*, (ACM, New York 2001) p. 408409

D.L. Kirkpatrick, *Evaluating Training Programs*, 2nd edn. (Berrett Koehler, San Francisco, 1959)

J. Klerkx, E. Duval, Visualising social bookmarks. J. Digital Inform. **10**(2), 1–40 (2009)

K. Koedinger, K. Cunningham, A. Skogsholm, B. Leber, An open repository and analysis tools for fine-grained, longitudinal learner data. in *Proceedings of Educational Data Mining 2008: 1st International Conference on Educational Data Mining*, ed by R.S.J.D. Baker, T. Barnes, J.E. Beck (Montreal, Quebec, Canada, 2008) June 20–21, pp. 157–166

K.R. Koedinger, R.S.J.D. Baker, K. Cunningham, A. Skogsholm, B. Leber, J. Stamper, A data repository for the EDM community: the PSLC datashop, in *Handbook of Educational Data Mining*, ed. by C. Romero, S. Ventura, M. Pechenizkiy, R.S.J.D. Baker (CRC Press, Boca Raton, 2010)

R. Kohavi, R. Longbotham, D. Sommerfield, R.M. Henne, Controlled experiments on the web: survey and practical guide. Data Min. Knowl. Discov. **18**(1), 140–181 (2009)

D. Lemire, H. Boley, S. McGrath, M. Ball, Collaborative filtering and inference rules for context-aware learning object recommendation. Int. J. Interact. Technol. Smart Educ. **2**(3), 179–190 (2005)

P. Lonsdale,C. Baber, M. Sharples, W. Byrne, P. Brundell, R. Beale, (2004) Context awareness for MOBIlearn: Creating an engaging learning experience in an art museum. In: MLEARN 2004, pp. 115–118

N. Manouselis, R. Vuorikari, F. Van Assche, Collaborative recommendation of e-learning resources: an experimental investigation. J. Comput. Assist. Learn. **26**(4), 227–242 (2010)

N. Manouselis, H. Drachsler, R. Vuorikari, H. Hummel, R. Koper, Recommender Systems in Technology Enhanced Learning, in *Recommender Systems Handbook*, ed by P. Kantor, F. Ricci, L. Rokach, B. Shapira (Springer, USA, 2011), pp. 387–415

H. Ogata, Y. Yano, Context-aware support for computer-supported ubiquitous learning, in *Proceedings of the 2nd IEEE International Workshop on Wireless and Mobile Technologies in Education (WMTE04)*, (IEEE Computer Society, Washington, DC, 2004), pp. 27–36

I. Okoye, K. Maull, J. Foster, T. Sumner, (2012) Educational recommendation in an informal intentional learning system. in *Educational Recommender Systems and Technologies: Practices and. Challenges*, ed by O. Santos, J. Boticario, pp. 1–23. doi:10.4018/978-1-61350-489-5.ch001

A. Paramythis, A. Totter, C. Stephanidis, A modular approach to the evaluation of adaptive user interfaces. in *Empirical Evaluation of Adaptive Systems* ed by S. Weibelzahl, D.N. Chin, G. Weber. in *Proceedings of workshop at the Eighth International Conference on User Modeling, UM2001*, (Freiburg, Germany, 2001) p. 924,

M. Recker, A. Walker, K. Lawless, What do you recommend? Implementation and analyses of collaborative filtering of Web resources for education. Instr. Sci. **31**(4/5), 229–316 (2003)

C. Reffay, M.-L. Betbeder, Sharing Corpora and Tools to Improve Interaction Analysis, in *Proceedings of EC-TEL '09, LNCS*, ed. by U. Cress, V. Dimitrova, M. Specht, vol. 5794, (Springer, Berlin, 2009), pp. 196–210

A. Said, S. Berkovsky, E.W. De Luca, Putting things in context: challenge on context-aware movie recommendation. in *Proceedings of the Workshop on Context-aware Movie Recommendation CAMRa '10*, ed by S. Berkovsky, E.W. De Luca, A. Said (Barcelona, Spain, 2010)

A. Said, S. Berkovsky, E.W. De Luca, J. Hermanns, Challenge on context-aware movie recommendation: CAMRa2011. in *Proceedings of the 5th ACM conference on Recommender systems (RecSys '11)*, (ACM, New York 2011)

A. Schmidt, Impact of context-awareness on the architecture of e-learning solutions, in *Architecture Solutions for E-Learning Systems, Chapter 16*, ed by C. Pahl (Information Science Reference, IGI Publishing, 2007), pp. 306–319

G. Shani, A. Gunawardana, Evaluating Recommendation Systems, in *Recommender Systems Handbook*, ed by F. Ricci, L. Rokach, B. Shapira (Springer USA, 2011), pp. 257–297

M.-A. Sicilia, E. Garca-Barriocanal, S. Snchez-Alonso, C. Cechinel, Exploring user-based recommender results in large learning object repositories: the case of MERLOT. in *Proceedings of the 1st Workshop on Recommender Systems for Technology Enhanced Learning (RecSysTEL 2010)*, N. Manouselis, H. Drachsler, K. Verbert, O.C. Santos. Procedia Comput. Sci. **1**(2), 2859–2864 (2010)

K. Swearingen, R. Sinha, Beyond algorithms: An HCI perspective on recommender systems. in *ACM SIGIR 2001 Workshop on Recommender Systems*, (2001) p. 11

N. Thai-Nghe, L. Drumond, A.R. Grimberghe, L. Schmidt-Thieme, Recommender system for predicting student performance. Procedia Comput. Sci. **1**(2), 2811–2819 (2010)

K. Verbert, H. Drachsler, N. Manouselis, M. Wolpers, R. Vuorikari, E. Duval, Dataset-driven research for improving recommender systems for learning. *Proceedings of the 1st International Conference on Learning Analytics and Knowledge*, (ACM, New York, 2011), pp. 44–53

K. Verbert, N. Manouselis, H. Drachsler, E. Duval, Dataset-driven research to support learning and knowledge analytics. Educ. Technol. Soci. Spec. Issue Learn. Knowl. Anal. (to appearA)

K. Verbert, N. Manouselis, O. Xavier, M. Wolpers, H. Drachsler, I. Bosnic, E. Duval, (to appearB) Context-aware recommender systems for learning: a survey and future challenges. IEEE Trans. Learn. Technol. Retrieved from https://lirias.kuleuven.be/handle/123456789/338644

S. Weibelzahl, Evaluation of adaptive systems. in *User Modeling: Proceedings of the Eighth International Conference, UM2001*, ed by M. Bauer, P.J. Gmytrasiewicz, J. Vassileva (Springer, Berlin, 2001), pp. 292294

S. Weibelzahl, A. Paramythis, A. Totter, A layered framework for the evaluation of interactive adaptive systems. in *2nd Workshop on Empirical Evaluation of Adaptive Systems, International Conference on User Modeling, UM2003*, (Johnstown, USA, 2003)

B. Xiao, I. Benbasat, E-commerce product recommendation agents: use, characteristics, and impact. MIS Q. **31**(1), 137–209 (2007)

V.A.R. Zaldivar, D. Burgos, Meta-Mender: A meta-rule based recommendation system for educational applications. Procedia Comput. Sci. **2**(1), 2877–2882 (2010). doi:10.1016/j.procs.2010.08.014.

V.A. Zaldivar, D. Burgos, A. Pardo, Meta-rule based recommender systems for educational applications. in *Educational Recommender Systems and Technologies: Practices and Challenges*, ed by O. Santos, J. Boticario. (2012), pp. 211–231. doi:10.4018/978-1-61350-489-5.ch009

S. Zhao, M.X. Zhou, Q. Yuan, X. Zhang, W. Zheng, R. Fu, Who is talking about what: social map-based recommendation for content-centric social websites. in *Proceedings of the 4th ACM Conference on Recommender Systems, RecSys10*, (ACM, New York, 2010), pp. 143–150

M. Zhou, Y. Xu, Challenges to use recommender systems to enhance meta-cognitive functioning in online learners. in *Educational Recommender Systems and Technologies:Practices and Challenges*, O. Santos, J. Boticario (2012), pp. 282–301. doi:10.4018/978-1-61350-489-5.ch012